KING HEDLEY II

August Wilson

THEATRE COMMUNICATIONS GROUP

NEW YORK

2005

This publication is made possible in part with public funds from the New York State Council on the Arts, a State Agency.

TCG books are exclusively distributed to the book trade by Consortium Book Sales and Distribution, 1045 Westgate Drive, St. Paul, MN 55114.

LIBRARY OF CONGRESS CATALOGING-IN-PUBLICATION DATA
Wilson, August.
King Hedley II / August Wilson.— 1st ed.
p. cm.
ISBN-10: 1-55936-260-X (pbk. : alk. paper) 1-55936-261-8 (cloth)
1. African American men—Drama. 2. Pittsburgh (Pa..)—Drama.
3. Ex-convicts—Drama.
I. Title: King Hedley the Second. II. Title.
PS3573.I45677K56   2005
812'.54—dc22   2005012535
ISBN-13: 978-1-55936-260-3

Text design by Lisa Govan
Cover design by John Gall
Cover image by Romare Bearden, *Pittsburg Memory*, 1964, collage on board, 8 1/2" x 11 3/4," collection of halley k harrisburg and Michael Rosenfeld
Author photo by David Cooper

First Edition, June 2005
Seventh Printing, August 2022

King Hedley II

For Rob Penny and Nicholas Flournoy
—fallen oaks of the Centre Avenue tradition

And for Chawley P. Williams
—don't you leave me here by myself

Preface

IN 1975 I WROTE A SHORT STORY titled "The Greatest Blues Singer in the World." As it turned out, the text of the story was very short. I began, "The streets that Balboa walked were his own private ocean, and Balboa was drowning." That seemed to communicate the idea with more clarity than I could hope to gain by adding to it, so I stopped and typed "The End."

I had conceived a much longer story that spoke to the social context of the artist and how one's private ocean is inextricably linked to the tributary streams that gave rise to, and occasioned, the impulse to song.

Before one can become an artist one must first *be*. It is *being* in all facets, its many definitions, that endows the artist with an immutable sense of himself that is necessary for the accomplishment of his task. Simply put, art is beholden to the kiln in which the artist was fired.

Before I am anything, a man or a playwright, I am an African American. The tributary streams of culture, history and experience have provided me with the materials out of which I make my art. As an African American playwright, I have many forebears who have pioneered and hacked out of the underbrush an aesthetic that embraced and elevated the cultural values of black Americans to a level equal to those of their European counterparts.

Out of their experiences, the sacred and the profane, was made a record of their traverse and the many points of epiphany and redemption. They have hallowed the ground and provided a tradition gained by will and daring. I count it a privilege to stand at the edge of the art, with the gift of their triumphs and failures, as well as the playwrights down through the ages who found within the turbulent history of human thought and action an ennobling conduct worthy of art. The culture of black America, forged in the cotton fields of the South and tested by the hard pavements of the industrial North, has been the ladder by which we have climbed into the New World. The field of manners and rituals of social intercourse—the music, speech, rhythms, eating habits, religious beliefs, gestures, notions of common sense, attitudes toward sex, concepts of beauty and justice, and the responses to pleasure and pain—have enabled us to survive the loss of our political will and the disruption of our history. The culture's moral codes and sanction of conduct offer clear instructions as to the value of community, and make clear that the preservation and promotion, the propagation and rehearsal of the value of one's ancestors is the surest way to a full and productive life.

The cycle of plays I have been writing since 1979 is my attempt to represent that culture in dramatic art. From the beginning, I decided not to write about historical events or the pathologies of the black community. The details of our struggle to survive and prosper, in what has been a difficult and sometimes bitter relationship with a system of laws and practices that deny us access to the tools necessary for productive and industrious life, are available to any serious student of history or sociology.

Instead, I wanted to present the unique particulars of black American culture as the transformation of impulse and sensibility into codes of conduct and response, into cultural rituals that defined and celebrated ourselves as men and women of high purpose. I wanted to place this culture onstage in all its richness and fullness and to demonstrate its ability to sustain us in all areas of human life and endeavor and through profound moments of our history in which the larger society has thought less of us than we have thought of ourselves.

From *Joe Turner's Come and Gone* (which is set in 1911) to *King Hedley II* (set in 1985), the cycle covers almost eighty years of American history. The plays are peopled with characters whose ancestors have been in the United States since the early seventeenth century.

They were brought across an ocean, chained in the hulls of 350-ton vessels. In the southern part of the United States, they were made to labor in the vast agricultural plantations. They made do without surnames and lived in dirt-floor cabins. They labored without pay. They were bought and sold and traded for money and gold and diamonds and molasses and horses and cows. They were fed the barest of subsistence diets. When they tried to escape, they were tracked down by dogs and men on horseback. They existed as an appendage to the body of society. They had no moral personality and no moral status in civic or church law.

After two-hundred-odd years, as a political expediency, they were granted freedom from being the property of other men. During the next hundred years they were disenfranchised, their houses were burned, they were hung from trees, forced into separate and inferior houses, schools and public facilities. They were granted status in law and denied it in practice.

Yet the characters in the plays still place their faith in America's willingness to live up to the meaning of her creed so as not to make a mockery of her ideals. It is this belief in America's honor that allows them to pursue the American Dream even as it remains elusive. The conflicts with the larger society are cultural conflicts. Conflicts over ways of being and doing things. The characters are all continually negotiating for a position, the high ground of the battlefield, from where they might best shout an affirmation of the value and worth of their being in the face of a many-million voice chorus that seeks to deafen and obliterate it.

They shout, they argue, they wrestle with love, honor, duty, betrayal; they have loud voices and big hearts; they demand justice, they love, they laugh, they cry, they murder, and they embrace life with zest and vigor. Despite the fact that the material conditions of their lives are meager. Despite the fact that they have no relationship with banking capital and their communities lack the twin pillars of commerce and industry. Despite the fact that their relationship to the larger society is one of servitude and marked neglect. In all the plays, the characters remain pointed toward the future, their pockets lined with fresh hope and an abiding faith in their own abilities and their own heroics.

From Herald Loomis's vision of the bones rising out of the Atlantic Ocean (the largest unmarked graveyard in the world) in *Joe Turner's Come and Gone*, to the pantheon of vengeful gods ("The Ghosts of the Yellow Dog") in *The Piano Lesson*, to Aunt Ester, the then 349-year-old conjure woman who first surfaced in *Two Trains Running*, the metaphysical presence of a spirit world has become increasingly important to my work. It is the world that the characters turn to when they are most in need.

Aunt Ester has emerged for me as the most significant persona of the cycle. The characters, after all, are her children. The wisdom and tradition she embodies are valuable tools for the reconstruction of their personality and for dealing with a society in which the contradictions, over the decades, have grown more fierce, and for exposing all the places it is lacking in virtue.

Theater, as a powerful conveyer of human values, has often led us through the impossible landscape of American class, regional and racial conflicts, providing fresh insights and fragile but enduring bridges of fruitful dialogue. It has provided us with a mirror that forces us to face personal truths and enables us to discover within ourselves an indomitable spirit that recognizes, sometimes across wide social barriers, those common concerns that make possible genuine cultural fusion.

With the completion of my latest play, *King Hedley II*, I have only the "bookends," the first and last decades of the twentieth century, remaining. As I approach the cycle's end, I find myself a different person than when I started. The experience of writing plays has altered me in ways I cannot yet fully articulate.

As with any journey, the only real question is: "Is the port worthy of the cruise?" The answer is a resounding: "Yes." I often remark that I am a struggling playwright. I'm struggling to get the next play on the page. Eight down and counting. The struggle continues.

This article first appeared in the New York Times, *April 23, 2000.*

King Hedley II

Production History

King Hedley II premiered at the Pittsburgh Public Theater on December 11, 1999, in association with Sageworks, in a co-production by the Pittsburgh Public Theater (Edward Gilbert, Artistic Director; Stephen Klein, Managing Director) and Seattle Repertory Theatre (Sharon Ott, Artistic Director; Benjamin Moore, Managing Director). The production subsequently opened at Seattle Repertory Theatre on March 13, 2000. The director was Marion Isaac McClinton; set design was by David Gallo, lighting design was by Donald Holder, sound design was by Rob Milburn and costume design was by Toni-Leslie James; the production stage manager was Diane DiVita. The cast was as follows:

KING HEDLEY II	Tony Todd
RUBY	Marlene Warfield
MISTER	Russell Andrews
ELMORE	Charles Brown
TONYA	Ella Joyce
STOOL PIGEON	Mel Winkler

This production of *King Hedley II* opened at Huntington Theatre Company (Peter Altman, Producing Director; Michael Maso, Managing Director) in Boston on May 24, 2000, with the same artistic team and cast, except for the following changes: original music was composed by Max Roach; the production stage manager was Glynn David Turner.

This production then opened at Mark Taper Forum (Gordon Davidson, Artistic Director; Charles Dillingham, Managing Director) in Los Angeles on September 5, 2000, with the same artistic team, except the production stage manager was Tami Toon. The cast was as follows:

KING HEDLEY II	Harry Lennix; Jerome Butler (October 17–22)
RUBY	Juanita Jennings
MISTER	Monté Russell
ELMORE	Charles Brown
TONYA	Moné Walton
STOOL PIGEON	Lou Myers

The production then opened at The Goodman Theatre (Robert Falls, Artistic Director; Roche Schuler, Executive Director) in Chicago on December 11, 2000, with the same artistic team, except the production stage manager was Diane DiVita. The cast was as follows:

KING HEDLEY II	Richard Brooks
RUBY	Leslie Uggams
MISTER	Monté Russell
ELMORE	Charles Brown
TONYA	Yvette Ganier
STOOL PIGEON	Lou Myers

The play opened at The John F. Kennedy Center for the Performing Arts in Washington, D.C., on February 25, 2001, with the same artistic team. It was produced by Sageworks, Benjamin Mordecai, Jujamcyn Theatres and Manhattan Theatre Club, in association with Kardana-Swinsky Productions. The cast was as follows:

KING HEDLEY II	Brian Stokes Mitchell
RUBY	Leslie Uggams
MISTER	Monté Russell
ELMORE	Charles Brown
TONYA	Viola Davis
STOOL PIGEON	Stephen McKinley Henderson

King Hedley II transferred to Broadway at the Virginia Theatre on May 1, 2001, with the same artistic team and cast. It was produced by Sageworks, Benjamin Mordecai, Jujamcyn Theaters, 52nd Street Productions, Spring Sirkin, Peggy Hill and Manhattan Theatre Club, in association with Kardana-Swinsky Productions.

Characters

KING (KING HEDLEY II), has a vicious scar running down the left side of his face. Spent seven years in prison. Strives to live by his own moral code. Thirties.

RUBY, King's mother, former big band singer who recently moved back to Pittsburgh. Sixties.

MISTER, King's best friend since grade school and sometimes business partner. Thirties.

ELMORE, Ruby's longtime, but sporadic flame. A professional hustler. Sixties.

TONYA, King's wife of a few years. Thirties.

STOOL PIGEON, King's next-door neighbor. The Hill's spiritual and practical truthsayer. Late sixties.

Setting

Pittsburgh, the Hill District, 1985. The setting is the backyards of a row of three houses. One of the houses is missing and the vacant lot provides access to the rear of the house where Ruby lives with King and Tonya. Three or four steps empty out of the house. A fence separates the yard from the house next door. Stool Pigeon lives in the house on the opposite side of the vacant lot. Buildings across the street in the front of the house are visible through the vacant lot and an old advertisement for Alaga Syrup featuring a faded portrait of Willie Mays is painted on one of the buildings.

Prologue

The lights come up on the yard. It is a brilliant, starry night lorded over by a calm that belies the approaching tempest. Stool Pigeon, sixty-five, enters from the house carrying two ham bones. He clicks them together. Offstage, a cat meows.

STOOL PIGEON: You stay out of the way of them dogs now. They gonna come for these bones.

(The cat meows.)

I'm gonna get you some fish heads tomorrow. I got to go down to the Strip District. Used to have the live fish market right down there on Center. Times ain't nothing like they used to be. Everything done got broke up. Pieces flying everywhere. Look like it's gonna be broke up some more before it get whole again. If it ever do. Ain't no telling. The half ain't never been told. The people don't know but God's gonna tell it. He gonna tell it in a loud voice. You ain't gonna be able to say you didn't hear it.

The people wandering all over the place. They got lost. They don't even know the story of how they got from tit to tat. Aunt Ester know. But the path to her house is all grown over with weeds, you can't hardly find the door no more. The people need to know that. The people need to know the story. See how they fit into it. See what part they play.

It's all been written down. We all have our hands in the soup and make the music play just so. But we can only make it play just so much. You can't play in the chord God ain't wrote. He wrote the beginning and the end. He let you play around in the middle but he got it all written down. It's his creation and he got more right in it than anybody else. He say, "Let him who have wisdom understand." Aunt Ester got the wisdom. She three hundred and sixty-six years old. She got the Book of Life. The story's been written. All that's left now is the playing out. (*He exits*)

(*The lights go down on the scene.*)

Act One

The lights come up on the yard. King Hedley II enters from the street. He is thirty-six years old and has a vicious scar running down the left side of his face. He goes to a small corner of the yard. He takes a packet of seeds from his pocket and begins to plant them. Ruby, sixty-one, enters from the house.

RUBY: When you gonna get the phone back on? You need a telephone.

KING: Soon as I get two hundred twenty-five dollars.

RUBY: I told Tonya I can go down and put it in my name.

KING: You ain't gonna get my phone on in your name. I'll wait till I get the two hundred and twenty-five dollars. What that look like, having my phone in your name?

RUBY: At least you would have a phone. You can't be without a phone.

KING: I don't need no phone, woman.

RUBY: I thought you was going back to work today.

KING: They didn't give Hop the contract. They was supposed to give him the contract to tear down that hotel in East

Liberty. He had the lowest bid but they didn't give him the contract. Now he got to go to court. He's having a hearing on Thursday.

RUBY: How come they didn't give him the contract?

KING: They said his bid was too low. Say he don't know what he doing. He been tearing buildings down his whole life and all of a sudden he don't know what he doing. They just afraid he gonna make a little bit of money. You got the lowest bid, you supposed to get the contract. They set up the rules and then don't want to follow them themselves.

RUBY: I got a letter from Elmore. He say he coming. Say he want to see you. Don't you be gambling with him when he come. You'll lose all your money.

KING: You ain't got to tell me about gambling with Elmore. He got all my money from the last time. He sold me that watch that quit working as soon as he walked out the door. You ain't got to tell me about Elmore. I know how he do. When he coming?

RUBY: He didn't say.

KING: What he wanna see me about?

RUBY: He say he want to see if you learned anything from being in jail. What you got there? What you doing?

KING: These some seeds. I'm gonna grow Tonya some flowers.

RUBY: You need some good dirt. Them seeds ain't gonna grow in that dirt.

KING: Ain't nothing wrong with this dirt.

RUBY: Get you some good dirt and put them seeds in it if you want them to grow. Your daddy knew what dirt was. He'd tell you you need some good dirt.

KING: This the only dirt I got. This is me right here.

RUBY: You stubborn just like him. You two of a kind. He couldn't get that Jamaican out of him. If he had did that he would have been all right.

KING: Haitian. He wasn't no Jamaican. He was Haitian.

RUBY: Haitian. Jamaican. They all the same. He was from the islands. What you and Mister up to? Tonya said you was selling refrigerators. You all out there stealing refrigerators, you goin' back to jail.

KING: See, there you go. You don't know where we getting them from. We selling them. We ain't stole them.

RUBY: Somebody stole them.

KING: I ain't asked the man where he got them from. He say do I want to sell some refrigerators. I ain't asked him where he got them from. I asked how much he was gonna pay me.

RUBY: What kind is they?

KING: They GE refrigerators. That's the best refrigerator on the market. Mellon got a GE refrigerator.

RUBY: You going back to jail. The police gonna find out. The police know everything.

KING: They don't know everything. They know where the whorehouse is and who sell the liquor after hours. But they don't know everything. They ain't God.

RUBY: What they don't know they find out.

KING: They ain't found out who killed Little Buddy Will in that drive-by on Bryn Mawr Road. His mama find out before they do. 'Cause she out there looking. They ain't found out who set that house on fire when them niggers tried to move out there in Shadyside.

RUBY: You watch what I'm saying. That's why they got the jail full, 'cause they find out who done what. That's their job to find out.

KING: They can find out all they want. I ain't done nothing. Leave me go with my business, woman. When you leaving? It's been two months since Louise died. You come here, call yourself taking care of her. You just come to see what you can get. Talked her into leaving you the house. Now that you got that, why don't you just go on.

RUBY: You watch yourself now. I told you the house was always in my name. It was never Louise's house. I give her the money for the house when I was singing. I sent her every month.

KING: That was money for her taking care of me.

RUBY: You don't know what it was for. Me and Louise had an understanding. I give her money for the house and I give her money for you. You don't know what went on between me and Louise. You don't know nothing about what happened between us.

KING: I just want to know when you leaving. That's all you can tell me. It's going on three months now.

RUBY: You know what I'm waiting on. As soon as I get the money from the city for the house, I'm leaving.

KING: They got a senior-citizen high-rise right up the street. You can move tomorrow.

RUBY: They got a waiting list. Got over two hundred people on the waiting list. Besides, you got to be on Social Security. I'll be sixty-two next month. I can get my Social Security and won't have to ask nobody for nothing. The city was supposed to let me know how much they was going to give me for the house last week. I told you I was going to give you half of what they give me.

KING: I don't want you to give me nothing. If Hop get that contract, I'm moving. I'm liable to move to California. That way I won't have to put up with you.

RUBY: You watch yourself. I'm still your mama.

KING: My mama dead. Louise my mama. That's the only mama I know.

RUBY: I done told you now.

KING: Where's Tonya?

RUBY: She in the house getting ready.

KING: Tell her to come on.

(Mister enters. He dresses neat, his shoes are always shined and he wears a hat. He is always polite and mannerly and has an easy and quick smile. He also carries a 9-mm pistol.)

MISTER: Hey, King.

RUBY: Hey, Mister!

MISTER: How you doing, Miss Ruby?

RUBY: Give me two dollars. I need to get me some beer.

MISTER: I ain't got no money right now. I ain't got paid yet. They got a crowd of people standing out in front of Aunt Ester's house. I started to go up there and find out what was going on. Aunt Ester's cat still watching that hole. Been up there two days now. I don't know how it can sit there that long.

KING: If it want that rat bad enough it will sit there till it come out.

MISTER: What you doing all dressed up? Where you going?

KING: Who said I was dressed up? Why I got to be dressed up?

MISTER: 'Cause you is.

KING: How many of the refrigerators you sold?

MISTER: I ain't sold but one. I need me one of them brochures. If I had one of them brochures I could sell a whole lot more. The people want to see what they look like.

KING: I told you I ain't got but one. Here . . . here . . . you take it! (*He hands Mister the brochure*)

MISTER: What model is it?

KING: Tell them you can get any model. What you care? They ain't gonna know the difference. If they do, just tell them it was a mistake. It ain't like they can take it back to the store. Don't tell them you can get the model that make ice, though. That's the only one we ain't got.

RUBY: I done told King . . . you better watch yourself. You all gonna end up in jail.

MISTER: We ain't doing nothing, Miss Ruby. We businessmen. We salesmen. We appliance salesmen. They might want us to go down to Philadelphia and sell some refrigerators down there. Then we be traveling salesmen.

KING: I might be able to sell some out in East Liberty. I'm taking Tonya to get her picture taken for our anniversary. High school ain't the only one make pictures. Sears make them every day.

MISTER: I always wanted to have my picture taken. You know how you have your picture taken when you pose for it. I thought that would make you somebody. I posed for the police. They told me I wasn't nothing but a sorry-ass criminal. I say, "Okay, just take my picture." They took my picture and I asked the man could I order some for my family and that was the beginning of all the trouble. They put me in the hole for trying to be smart. He don't know I was serious.

RUBY: What they had you down the jail for. Stealing something?

MISTER: Now, Miss Ruby . . . you ain't never know me to steal nothing.

RUBY: What they have you down there for? That's what most people down there for.

MISTER: They said I stole some TVs. But I didn't do it. Ask King. I knew who done it but I wouldn't tell them. They tried to make it like I did it. The judge threw it out when it come to trial.

RUBY: I know you stole them. I'm just telling you to watch yourself. You and King both.

MISTER: We ain't doing nothing, Miss Ruby.

KING: Hey Mister, do I have a halo around my head?

MISTER: A what?

KING: A halo. Do you see a halo around my head?

MISTER: You ain't got no halo. The devil looking for you and you talking about a halo.

KING: I had this dream last night. I dreamt I had a halo.

MISTER: I dreamt I had a pocketful of money. You see how far that got me. I had so much money I couldn't walk right. They had to put me in a wheelbarrow. I woke up and was still broke.

KING: Naw, I'm serious. I dreamt I had a halo. The police was chasing me and all of a sudden they stopped and just looked at me. I said, "It must be my halo," only I didn't know if it was there or not.

MISTER: I don't know if it's there or not either. Hey Miss Ruby, do you see a halo around King's head?

RUBY: Anybody get their dreams mixed up with real life is headed for Mayview. He gonna beat Stool Pigeon there.

MISTER: Stool Pigeon almost got shot yesterday. People don't like him coming in their yards and taking the lid off the garbage cans so the dogs can eat. One man took a shot at him. Right up there on Webster.

KING: I bet that's one yard he won't go in again.

RUBY: That old fool taking the lids off the garbage cans got all these rats around here. I done told him they gonna put him in Mayview. He wasn't right in 1948 when I met him. And he ain't right now. Got all them papers stacked up over there. You watch and see if they don't put him in Mayview.

KING *(To Ruby)*: Where Tonya? Tell her to come on if she going. What she doing in there? Tell her to come on.

RUBY *(Calls)*: Tonya! *(She exits into the house)*

MISTER: Hey King, I heard Pernell's cousin's looking for you?

KING: Who? Who's Pernell's cousin?

MISTER: You seen him. He drive a red Buick. Got some light-skinned girl he go around with. He got a goatee. And he wear a yellow hat. Always got on a dark shirt. Riding around in a red Buick with a fake telephone. Look like he done hit the numbers or something.

KING: He got an earring in his ear?

MISTER: That's him!

KING: That's Pernell's cousin?

MISTER: They ran him out of Pittsburgh about ten years ago. He shot them two men out in Homewood Park. Two brothers. Got in an argument over a football game. One of them still walk around crippled. He's back in Pittsburgh now. Came back after Pernell's mother died.

KING: I don't care nothing about him.

MISTER: He care something about you. That's what he be talking. How you done killed Pernell and he never had a chance at life. How you cheated him out of that.

KING: Fuck Pernell!

MISTER: That's what somebody told me he said.

KING: Have a chance at what? What Pernell had a chance at? I never met a nigger that was dumber than him. Anybody flunk the third grade ain't got too much going for them. What chance he have? That show you how dumb Pernell's cousin is. Talking about I cheated him out of a chance at life. The nigger cut my face!

MISTER: He done put it out that he looking for you. He going all around talking about it. He talking blood for blood. You got to watch yourself. You know how Pernell was. His cousin just like him. Pernell was just like his daddy. They was two of a kind.

KING: Them was some sneaky motherfuckers. Him and his daddy both. I'm glad they both dead.

MISTER: They whole family's sneaky.

(Tonya and Ruby enter. Tonya is thirty-five years old. She is wearing a yellow blouse.)

TONYA: How this look?

MISTER: You look nice. I like that yellow.

TONYA: Natasha think she smart. I told her about wearing my clothes. She done took my red blouse over to my mother's. Got my makeup and everything. She don't know she on borrowed time with me. I was gonna wear my red blouse.

RUBY: I told her she don't need no red.

MISTER: Hey Tonya, I want to get one of them pictures. I'm gonna show everybody and tell them you my sister. Sears got real good color too. They make their pictures look real clear.

RUBY: Sure do. Natasha's pictures turned out real nice.

MISTER: Natasha got them big eyes. The baby look just like her. How she doing? The last time I seen her she had blond streaks in her hair.

TONYA: She over my mother's. I had to send her over there. She think she grown. She don't know what she doing. Said she was going back to school but she change her mind every other week. She was going to hairdressing school but she quit that. Now she's gonna join the Navy. Next week it'll be something else. She don't know what she doing.

MISTER: Hey Tonya, do you see a halo around King's head? He talkin' he dreamt he had a halo. I told him he woke now.

KING: You don't know. I might have dreamt it 'cause it's true.

TONYA: If he did have one it's gone now.

RUBY: I told him he gonna end up in Mayview.

KING: Hey Mister, guess who's coming? Elmore. He say he coming to see what I learned.

RUBY: He need to stay where he at.

MISTER: Hey King, you remember that watch?

KING: Yeah I remember. I'm gonna get Elmore for that.

MISTER: Elmore sold King a watch that quit running two days later.

RUBY: I told King don't you all be gambling with Elmore when he come. You'll lose all your money.

MISTER: I'm gonna get me some crooked dice too. I'm gonna start practicing and be ready when he come. I know how to cheat, too.

RUBY: Elmore got a way with gambling. He don't need to cheat. You'll lose all your money if you gamble with him. I'm telling you.

MISTER: I'm gonna get me some dice and be ready for him. When he coming? Where he at? Last time he was out in California.

KING: I don't know. Hey, Ruby, where the letter? What the letter say?

RUBY: Talking about he a new man. (*She takes a letter out of her pocket and tries to read it*) Here, Tonya, read this. My glasses in the house. (*She hands the letter to Tonya*)

TONYA (*Reads*): Dear Ruby, I know we have had some problems when last I seen you, but I do believe you will be glad to see me as I am sure I will be. You have a hold on me. (Smile.) I am on my way to Cleveland and Pittsburgh is my favorite as I have had a lot of good times. Do you know any gamblers? If so, tell them to get ready as they will surely lose all their money. My oldest boy, Robert, is in the Army and is a sergeant. You remember he liked to play with guns. He says he will make a career. Tell King I am coming to see him. I know he have had some hard times. I want to see if he have learned anything. (*King exits into the house. Tonya continues reading the letter*) I guess I will close for now. In a few days I will show you that I miss you, and if you think, you will see that the good times have always outweighed the bad times. My mother died last year and she always remembered you as I have. Look for me and you will see that I am a new man. Your pal, Elmore.

(*Tonya hands Ruby the letter. Ruby folds it and puts it back in her pocket.*)

RUBY: I don't know why he can't stay where he's at. It ain't never nothing good with him. On one side it seem like he's all right but he'll turn on you every time. He'll flip that other side over on you in a minute. He talk sugar but give salt. 'Cause they both look the same, he don't even know it. He ain't the one that taste it. He need to stay where he's at. I'm getting too old for all this.

TONYA: Tell him not to come.

RUBY: Elmore don't listen to nobody. He don't pay no attention to what you say. He play at good manners but it ain't real. Something's always missing with him. There's always something he ain't got. He don't know what it is himself. If you gave it to him, he wouldn't know he had it. I see him every four or five years. He come on through and always leave more trouble than when he came. Seem like he bring it with him and dump it off. He come and dump off that trouble and then walk out smelling sweet.

MISTER: Ain't nothing wrong with Elmore. Elmore got some style. And he got class.

RUBY (*To Mister*): He got some trouble he wanna dump off too. Where your wife? I ain't seen her in a while.

MISTER: My wife took all the furniture and left me. I'm scared to love somebody else.

RUBY: What she leave you for? I know you ain't hit her.

MISTER: She try to get me to change. I was gonna hit her but I changed my mind. She left 'cause I wasn't like she wanted me to be. But she ain't looking at that's what made her like me. I'm thinking she liked me for being me. Come to find out she wanted me to change. The first time I saw her, I knew I was in trouble.

RUBY: You probably was in love and didn't know it. The first time you seen her I bet you was in love.

MISTER: It don't last. First thing you know, she do something to mess it up. We was together four years. I had sixty-seven hopes and dreams but she messed it up.

TONYA: How she mess it up? She might have had a hundred hopes and dreams.

RUBY: You probably ain't treated her right.

MISTER: I treated her better than anybody else gonna treat her. She gonna find that out.

(King enters from the house with a Glock 9-mm pistol. He shoves the clip in the gun.)

KING: Pernell's cousin talking about he looking for me. Naw, I'm looking for him. I want to see him tell me that shit about cheating Pernell out of a chance at life. Come on, Tonya, if you going. Tonya, come on.

(King starts out of the yard. Stool Pigeon enters in a rush.)

STOOL PIGEON: Lock your doors! Close your windows! Turn your lamp down low! We in trouble now. Aunt Ester died! She died! She died! She died!

(The lights go down on the scene.)

SCENE 2

The lights come up on the yard. King is watering his seeds. Stool Pigeon, carrying two jugs of water, enters from the house.

KING: Hey, Stool Pigeon.

STOOL PIGEON: You hear that wind last night? That was God riding through the land. We in trouble now. These niggers don't know but God got a plan. The Bible say, "I will call the righteous out of the land. I will gather thee to thy grave in peace; and thine eyes shall not see all the evil that I will bring upon this place."

KING: Sound like he talking about Aunt Ester.

STOOL PIGEON: He had to get her out of the way before he bring the fire.

KING: Them people still up there standing around her house.

STOOL PIGEON: They been up there ever since the word got out about her dying. The Bible say to mourn for three days. Some people say you supposed to wait till they put the body in the ground. They done started their three days already.

KING: I went up and asked Mr. Eli. I'm gonna be a pallbearer.

STOOL PIGEON: I'm going up there and take the people these blankets. I'm gonna see if he want me to do anything.

KING: Hey, Stool Pigeon. Do you see a halo around my head?

STOOL PIGEON: Aunt Ester's the one to ask about that. But it's too late now. She's gone. She ain't here no more. Aunt Ester knew all the secrets of life but that's all gone now. She took all that with her. I don't know what we gonna do. We in trouble now.

KING: Look at this. That's a gold key ring Aunt Ester gave me. I used to cut her grass and keep the path clear. One day she come out on the porch and gave me that key ring.

STOOL PIGEON: "And the people went out and made idols and graven images of gold and silver in blasphemy against the Lord, and the key was given unto the righteous that they might enter the kingdom for the scourge was upon the land and the wrath of the Lord God Jehovah was visited upon every house." You see, the key belongs to the righteous. Aunt Ester gave you the key ring, that means you got to find the key.

KING: Mr. Eli say she died from grief.

STOOL PIGEON: Died with her hand stuck to her head. She ain't seen nothing but grief. After three hundred and sixty-six years it ganged up on her. These niggers think it's a joke. But they don't know. The Spirit of God went out upon the waters and it commenced to rain. For forty days and forty nights. God already done that. He don't have to do that no more. He say next time he gonna come with the fire. Say he will bring it down upon the earth with a vengeance. I had a preacher say that once. "God will bring down fire on the earth with a vengeance." He say, "You know what that mean?" Everybody say, "Amen." He kept asking so I figured he wanted to know. He say, "You know what that mean?" So I stood up and said, "Yeah, that mean He gonna fuck it up." They threw me out the church. For telling the truth!

KING: I went down to the drugstore and get Aunt Ester her medicine every week. Seem like it didn't do her no good.

STOOL PIGEON: God got a plan. That medicine can't go against God. God do what He want to do. He don't have to ask nobody nothing. Say, "I will call the righteous out of the land and raise up in thy midst a Messiah from amongst my people to redeem thy iniquities and He shall by the remission of blood make whole that which is torn asunder even though it be scattered to the four winds, for Great is My Name and ye shall know by these signs the coming of a new day." See. He talking about the Messiah. He had to get Aunt Ester out of the way. God got a plan.

MISTER (Entering from the street): Hey, King. Hey, Stool Pigeon. Are your lights still out?

KING: They supposed to have them back on today.

STOOL PIGEON: They went out all over the city when Aunt Ester died. She died and all the lights went out. God got a plan.

MISTER: Them people still up there on the corner in front of Aunt Ester's house.

STOOL PIGEON: They ain't going nowhere. They gonna be standing up there until they put her body in the ground. I'm taking them some water before I go down to Pat's Place to get my papers. (*He exits*)

KING: I thought you was at work.

MISTER: I called in late.

KING: If I was you, I would have been done quit. You was supposed to get a raise three months ago. Go down there and tell them people to give you a raise.

MISTER: They say they got to wait till they get some orders.

KING: That ain't your fault. If they can't get no business, tell them to close down. You working every day.

MISTER: We got a big order coming in this week. I'm gonna wait and see. You see Pernell's cousin?

KING: I went down to the 88 looking for him. I didn't see him. Somebody say he be up on Herron Avenue. I went up there and didn't see him.

MISTER: Sometime he be out in Homewood.

KING: I'm goin' out there and look for him. When I find him, that'll be the last time we see each other.

(*He points to a small, barely discernible spot of green growing where he planted the seeds*) Look at that. See that growing. See that!

MISTER: Yeah, I see.

KING: Ruby tell me my dirt ain't worth nothing. It's mine. It's worth it to have. I ain't gonna let nobody take it. Talking about I need some good dirt. Like my dirt ain't worth nothing. A seed is a seed. A seed will grow in dirt. Look at that!

MISTER: Yeah, I see.

KING: How many of them refrigerators you sell?

MISTER: I sold two more. One man owe me fifty dollars. He say he gonna pay me on Tuesday. How many you sell?

KING: I sold three. That make seven. We ain't got but four more days to sell as many as we can, then they gonna move them down to Philadelphia and we be done missed our opportunity.

MISTER: I be asking everybody.

KING: You just ain't asked the right people.

MISTER: It ain't like they TVs. TVs would be easier.

KING: This better than TVs. Everybody already got a TV. But everybody be thinking about getting a new refrigerator. Only they don't never get around to it. That's when you walk up and offer them a brand-new GE refrigerator for two hundred dollars. That make you a hero. People be seeing you ten years from now smile when they see you. They don't never forget where they got that refrigerator from.

MISTER: Hey King, I was thinking . . . I want to get my money out the pot. I need to get me some furniture.

KING: Naw, naw. We supposed to get the video store! We split the pot and there won't be nothing to get it with. We got around six thousand dollars. We don't need but four more. I ain't gonna be poor all my life. See, you don't believe it.

MISTER: I believe it. I just need me some furniture.

KING: I need too! I need two hundred and twenty-five dollars to get my phone back on. Natasha talked to some nigger from Baltimore for six hours. I need, too, but you don't hear me talking about dipping in the pot. See, 'cause I believe. I look at that sign say "Miller Auto Parts." Niggers don't believe it can say "Hedley Auto Parts." Or "Carter Auto Parts." Or you can have one say "Royal Videos." How you think Miller got that auto-parts store? 'Cause he didn't dip in the pot.

MISTER: I need to get me some money. We can get the video store later. I just want my money. It's been sitting in the pot all that time. I don't even know where the pot is. You say you got it but I ain't seen it. I just want my money.

KING: We already talked to the man about renting the place. He say to come back when we ready. We almost ready. Now you talking about splitting the pot. You want your money. That's why niggers ain't got nothing now. They don't believe!

MISTER: I just want my money. I need it. I got to get me some furniture.

KING: I need the money from the refrigerators to get my phone back on. Tonya pregnant. She want a car. I got to buy a crib. A stroller. Got to figure out how to get Ruby one of these refrigerators. I got the light bill. The gas bill. Got to get some food. But I ain't said nothing about splitting the pot. You supposed to pretend like it ain't there.

MISTER: I didn't know Tonya was pregnant.

KING: I just found out myself. Remember when we used to play touch football and everybody looking at me and we'd do that double reverse and I'd hand off to you.

MISTER: That was a touchdown every time.

KING: I used to tell Neesi I wanted to have a baby. Wanted somebody to hand off the ball to. Took me all this time. Now Tonya pregnant. It's like I finally did something right. That's why you got to leave your money in the pot. I don't want him to grow up without nothing.

MISTER: I'm supposed to get a raise on my job but I can't count on that. I need someplace to sleep. I just want my money. We can start another pot later.

KING: Okay. Okay. That jewelry store we was talking about and I told you I didn't want to do that.

MISTER: Down there on Fifth Avenue by Tobin's Distributors? I told you we can take that easy. Might get around twenty or thirty thousand. The least would be around ten thousand.

KING: Leave your money in the pot. We hit that jewelry store, we have enough to get the video store and you can still get some furniture.

MISTER: All right. When you wanna do it? We got to do it soon. I need me some furniture. I can take off work Wednesday. That's as good a time as any. Wednesday a slow day.

KING: All right. We'll do it Wednesday. Where Deanna go? Over to her mother's?

MISTER: Yeah, she over there. She bumped into a door and told her mother I hit her. Her mother called me up threatening me.

KING: That's what mothers supposed to do. You think she gonna call you up and talk sweet to you? Mothers look out for their kids. That's why Little Buddy Will's mother is out there in the street with her nine-millimeter looking for whoever killed her son. Mothers supposed to threaten you. Just make sure she ain't hanging around your front doorstep.

MISTER: Her mother might have her boyfriend come after me. I don't know. But you know I'm always ready for whatever go down.

KING: You just be ready to sell some more refrigerators.

MISTER: I sold more than you.

KING: I said just be ready to sell some more. We hit that jewelry store, I can put my life back in order. Only thing, I got to get Neesi off my mind. Every day it be the same. I can't carry her no more. It hurts. I thought Tonya would help. She made it worse. She showed me a lot of woman. All the woman she could be. I told myself I ain't gonna measure it. I ain't gonna measure one against the other. They really about the same. Only thing, I can't get Neesi off my mind. That's my one wish.

MISTER: That be hard. Maybe if you don't try and put her off your mind, she'll go away. Like I can't remember a lot of things 'cause I ain't trying to forget them. If I was trying to forget them they be on my mind. Either that or they got some medicine make you forget things. Only thing with that is sometimes you forget your name.

KING: I'll try anything but I don't think it'll work. I went out and visited her grave yesterday. I feel like there's something I want to tell her but I don't know what it is. I was just thinking about the way she made me laugh. She'd say something and make it like she was joking with me, like it was good to be alive and she was just discovering that. Ain't too many people make me laugh. A lot more of them would make me want to kill. She made me do both. She was funny like that. She'd give you the strength, like you say, "I'm gonna kill Pernell," and the next thing you say is, "No, I ain't gonna kill him," and then she just look at you like you was King of the

World and that's when you say, "Yeah, I can kill him and kill him good." That's the way she was. She turned state's evidence and I didn't laugh for a long while.

MISTER: She got scared and the police tricked her. She thought they was going to put her in jail.

KING: I know. I don't blame her. She blamed herself but she knew I didn't blame her.

MISTER: Neesi was special.

KING: I used to tell her I'd give her her weight in gold if she just whisper my name.

MISTER: I felt real bad when I heard she got killed in that car crash.

KING: They wouldn't even let me go to the funeral. Talking about she wasn't family.

MISTER: I know. I put a rose in her casket for you.

KING: Hey, we got the lights back.

(Stool Pigeon enters carrying a bundle of newspapers.)

STOOL PIGEON (Reading newspaper): "House Collapses in West End."

KING: Hey, Stool Pigeon.

STOOL PIGEON (Showing them a newspaper): God knocking down houses! He got Aunt Ester out the way and now he knocking down houses. Soon he gonna come with the fire.

MISTER: That's the wind blowing down that house.

STOOL PIGEON: God tell the wind what to do! He say, "Go blow that house down," and the wind go blow it down. You think Peter Wolf was bad! He blow down the sticks and the straw. When it come to the brick he can't do nothing with it. But God can blow down the brick! You ever see it get so hot you can fry an egg on the sidewalk? That's God frying that egg! God's a bad motherfucker! He tell the sun and the moon what to do. You think the devil do that? The devil have a hard enough time trying to get your black ass to do something. Most times you have to hear the devil twice.

God say something and you come to attention right away. He knocking down houses now but soon he gonna come with the fire. God's a bad motherfucker.

MISTER: Why you save all them newspapers? What you gonna do with them?

STOOL PIGEON: See I know what went on. I ain't saying what goes on . . . what went on. You got to know that. How you gonna get on the other side of the valley if you don't know that? You can't guess on it . . . you got to know. Look at that. (*He shows them another newspaper*) "Man Bludgeons School-teacher." See? You got to know that. "City's Tax Levy Challenged." See? You got to know that. Some people don't mind guessing . . . but I got to know. If you want to know, you can ask me and I'll go look it up. The valley's got a lot of twists and turns. You can get lost in the daytime! Look at that: "Man Stabs Assailant." See? You got to know that. If you don't, you gonna find out soon enough.

(*Ruby enters from the house.*)

RUBY: You old buzzard! Go on in the house!

STOOL PIGEON: I don't want you, woman!

RUBY: Go on in the house! You need to throw them papers out. Can't even walk in there.

STOOL PIGEON: You mind your business now.

RUBY: This is my business. I'm going down to Pat's Place and tell them to stop saving them papers for you. I don't know why they give them to you. That's a firetrap. I'm gonna tell your landlord you got all them papers stored in there. If he don't do nothing I'm gonna call right down there to the city. They gonna send the fire inspector.

STOOL PIGEON: I ain't studying you, woman. The Bible say your enemies cannot harm you. Say, "He that set his tongue against you shall I cause to rue all his misspoken words for a lie maketh the tongue swell with folly and the taste shall be as bile and a bitter reward shall be his just dessert." That's in the Bible! Roman 14:12. You know what that means, don't you? That means you can go to hell! *(He exits into his house)*

RUBY: You can't even walk in there. He got all them papers stacked all over the place. You got to turn sideways. He think I'm playing but I am gonna call down there to the city. They don't allow that. They had that woman had sixty-seven cats. They made her get rid of them and if I call down there to the city they gonna make him get rid of them papers. King, give me twenty dollars to get Aunt Ester some flowers.

KING: You can't get no flowers for twenty dollars.

RUBY: Give me thirty then. I want to get her some flowers. She was real nice to me.

KING: I ain't got no thirty dollars. I'm trying to get the phone back on.

MISTER: I'll loan you thirty dollars, Miss Ruby. When you gonna pay me back?

RUBY: When I get it. I can't pay you otherwise.

(Mister gives Ruby thirty dollars.)

MISTER: Could you put my name on there too?

RUBY: I would. But this is something special between me and Aunt Ester. She was real nice to me.

MISTER: I got to get on to work. We got some orders we got to get out this week. Hey King, I'm gonna take off Wednesday and we can take care of our business.

RUBY: What you all got to do Wednesday? You all up to something.

KING: This my business, woman. Why don't you leave me go with my business. You ain't got to watch over me. You wasn't watching over me when you took off to East St. Louis and left me here with Mama Louise. You wasn't watching over me then. I don't need you to tell me nothing. Your time to tell me done come and gone.

RUBY: You watch yourself now.

(There's a knock on the front door.)

Somebody knocking on my door. *(Calls)* Who is it? Who knocking on my door?

(Elmore enters. He is sixty-six years old. The consummate hustler, he is stylishly dressed, though his clothes are well-worn and his over-all look is a man whose life is fraying at the edges. Still, he exudes an air of elegance and confidence born of his many years wrestling with life. He stops and looks at Ruby. They look at each other a long while.)

ELMORE: Here I am, on your hands again.
RUBY: You ain't good for nothing.
ELMORE: How you doing, Ruby?
RUBY: I'm doing. I'm doing without you.
ELMORE: You look like you doing all right. Did you get my let-ter? *(He notices King)* Hey, King. Your mama tell you I was coming to see you?

(King and Elmore shake hands.)

KING: Hey Elmore, why you sell me that watch?
ELMORE: 'Cause you wanted to buy it. I wanna see you happy. I don't want to sell you nothing you don't want.
KING: That wasn't right.
ELMORE: How else you gonna learn? I bet you ain't bought no more.
RUBY: Where your suitcase?
ELMORE: They in the car.
RUBY: You can sleep on the couch.
KING: You remember Mister?
ELMORE: How you doing?

(Elmore and Mister shake hands.)

MISTER: I like that hat.

ELMORE: I got this in New York.

KING: Mister say he want to shoot some crap.

MISTER: I ain't got my dice yet.

ELMORE: I got some dice.

MISTER: Naw naw, we don't shoot no crap. We got us another thing going.

ELMORE: I told your mother if she knew any gamblers to let them know I was coming. I'm always looking for a crap game.

RUBY: That's the first thing come out his mouth. He can't even get in the door good before he looking for a crap game. Where my present? Why didn't you bring me a present?

ELMORE: I got it in the car. You know I got you a present. As many presents as I done give you. That's what I used to live for.

RUBY: That's what I say. I know you didn't come without a present. You got good manners. I know that.

KING: You want to buy a refrigerator? We selling refrigerators.

ELMORE: I don't need no refrigerator. No stove either. I'm traveling light.

RUBY: Come on in the house, let me fix you something to eat. I know you hungry. Come on, I'll fry you some chicken. (*She exits into the house*)

ELMORE: You selling refrigerators, huh?

KING: Yeah, me and Mister. How many you want to buy?

ELMORE: Where you get them from?

KING: Some white fellow I was in the penitentiary with ask me do I want to sell some refrigerators. I ain't asked him where he got them from, I just asked him how much he was gonna pay me.

ELMORE: How many you got?

KING: We got as many as you want. Different sizes. Some of them is great big twenty cubic.

MISTER: We sold sixteen already.

ELMORE: Where they at?

KING: I ain't saying where they at. They could be anywhere. The rail yard. In a truck. If I could have fit them upstairs they'd be up there. I ain't saying where they at. If you want to buy one I'll show you a picture.

ELMORE: I ain't said I want to buy one.

(King takes the brochure from Mister.)

KING: Look at that. Which one you want? I'll let you have any one for two hundred dollars. There's some models we ain't got. We ain't got that one make its own ice. It'll cost you four hundred if we had it.

ELMORE: I want to see these refrigerators.

KING: Naw . . . naw, we can't let you do that.

ELMORE: I don't believe you got them.

KING: That's all right. Put in your order and see how fast one of them turn up on your doorstep. Delivered free. Come to think of it, we should charge twenty dollars for the delivery.

ELMORE: I don't want to buy none. I was gonna help you sell them. I always say three salesman is better than two. That way you sell three times as much. How much you gonna give me if I sell one?

KING: We'll give you twenty-five dollars.

ELMORE: Make it thirty. I got to cover my overhead.

KING: What overhead you got, nigger? You ain't got no overhead.

ELMORE: I got to get me some gas. I use up all my gas riding around trying to find somebody to buy a refrigerator. Ain't no tell how much you got to ride around. Now if you had some TVs, that be a different thing.

MISTER: That's what I told him.

KING: Naw . . . You can sell a refrigerator just as quick as you can a TV. You might sell it quicker. The trick is to find somebody with two hundred dollars. If they could make payments they be all right. But this is two hundred dollars cash money.

ELMORE: Make it thirty. I got to pay for my gas.

KING: All right. Thirty. We got till Friday. Else they be gone.

MISTER: We can't let them sit in one place too long.

KING: We got till Friday to sell as many as we can.

MISTER: Then they going down to Philadelphia.

KING: We selling refrigerators right now but me and Mister gonna open up a video store. We almost got all the money.

MISTER: And we gonna get the rest soon.

ELMORE: I don't know nothing about no video store but if you get you a little place and sell some fried chicken and put you a gambling room in the back . . . then you got something there. I'll go in with you on something like that but I don't know nothing about no video store.

KING: That's all right. We know. We gonna call it Royal Videos.

MISTER: We gonna specialize in kung-fu movies.

KING: If everything go right, we liable to end up with Royal Videos in fifty states.

RUBY (*Calling from inside the house*): Elmore . . . come on.

KING: He's coming!

(*Stool Pigeon enters from his house with a bowl of chili and a newspaper. He sits on his steps and eats and reads.*)

STOOL PIGEON: Pirates winning four to two.

ELMORE: Who's that?

MISTER: That's Stool Pigeon. He don't bother nobody.

STOOL PIGEON: My name ain't Stool Pigeon. My name is Canewell. I try to tell these niggers that.

ELMORE: How you doing? I'm Elmore.

STOOL PIGEON: Yeah, I heard a lot about you.

MISTER: I got to get to work. Get me some money. The white man got all the money.

ELMORE: Money ain't nothing. I ain't had but a dollar sixty-seven cents when I met your mama. I had a hundred-dollar Stetson hat, a pint of gin and a razor. That and a dollar sixty-seven cents. I'm walking around with a hundred-dollar hat and a dollar and sixty-seven cents in my pocket. I told myself, "Something wrong. This ain't working out right." The razor was my daddy's razor. He had cut him eleven niggers with that razor. Had good weight to it. Felt nice in your hands. Make you wanna cut somebody. The pint of gin I had just borrowed from the after-hour joint. I stepped outside and saw her standing there. I asked her name and she told me. Told me say, "My name's Ruby." And somehow that fit her like she was a jewel or something precious. That's what I told her say, "You must be precious to somebody." She told me she ain't had nobody. We got to talking and one thing led to another. I took and spent a dollar sixty cents on her. Bought me a nickel cigar. Now I got a razor, a pint of gin, a hundred-dollar Stetson, a cigar, two cents and a woman. I was ready for whatever was out there. I woke up in the morning and felt lucky. Pawned my Stetson. Got seven dollars and went down the gambling joint. Playing dollar tonk. Left out of there broke. She back at my place waiting on me. I got to at least bring dinner. I looked up and seen a white fellow standing on the corner. He wasn't doing anything. Just standing there. Had on a gray hat. I told myself, "He got some money." I walked right on by. I didn't look at him. When I got even with him, I threw him up against the wall. I told myself I wasn't gonna use my razor unless I had to. He gave me his money and I started to run. I can't walk away. I'm running but I ain't running fast. I heard the bullet when it passed me. That's a sound I don't never want to hear again. You can hear the air move. When that bullet split the air, it make a sound. If you don't know I will tell you. You can fly. I was running so fast my feet wasn't touching the ground. Yet I moving through the air. What I'm doing? I'm flying. Ain't nothing else you can call it. I got away and told myself I was lucky. Then I knew why I had woke up feeling like that. When I got to where I could look in my hand to see what I had. I looked down and I had seven dollars. I told myself, hell, if I could get fifty cents I can go back and get my hat out of the pawn shop. Call it even. Start over again tomorrow.

RUBY (*Offstage*): Elmore!

STOOL PIGEON (*Showing newspaper*): Look at that! "City Violence Escalates. Teen Killed in Drive-By." You got to know that!

ELMORE: "Teen Killed in Drive-By." I'm tired of hearing that. See . . . a man has got to have honor. A man ain't got no honor can't be a man. He can only play at being a man. He can pretend to be a man. But if he ain't got no honor it'll tell on him every time. When the time come to be honorable you can't find him. Now what is honor? You ever seen that movie where this man goes to kill this other man and he got his back to him and he tell him to turn around so he can see his eyes? That's honor. A man got to have that else he ain't a man. You can't be no man stealing somebody's life from the backseat of a Toyota. That's why the black man's gonna catch hell for the next hundred years. These kids gonna grow up and get old and ain't a man among them.

KING: It used to be you get killed over something. Now you get killed over nothing.

MISTER: You might look at somebody wrong and get in a fight and get killed over that.

STOOL PIGEON: I seen a man get killed over a fish sandwich. Right down there at Cephus's. Had two fish sandwiches . . . one with hot sauce and one without. Somebody got them mixed up and these two fellows got to arguing over them. The next thing you know it was a surprise to God to find out that one of them had six bullet holes in him.

ELMORE: That's why I carry my pistol. They got too many fools out there.

KING: What you carrying?

ELMORE: I got me a Smith & Wesson .38 Special.

MISTER: King got a Glock. I told him a Beretta be better.

KING: Any gun will kill. It don't matter how pretty the gun and it don't matter what size the hole.

ELMORE: Everybody walking around with big .44s leave a hole in you the size of a cantaloupe. I tried one of them but it made my shoulder sore. I didn't want to end up crippled so

I went out and bought me a Smith & Wesson .38 Special in 1959 and I ain't been without it since. I'm a gunfighter. That stop somebody dead in his tracks.

STOOL PIGEON: You a gunfighter, but God's a firefighter. God got the fire. Your little old pistol can't stand up against God. The atomic bomb can't stand up against God. He say, "I will smite my enemies. I will make battlefields out of the pastures and send a rain of fire on the earth so that all may know I am the Alpha and the Omega, the beginning and the end. Numberless are my wonders and my vengeance is twice-fold." Twice-fold! God is a motherfucker!

ELMORE: Let's leave God out of it. God ain't got nothing to do with it. We ain't talking about God. We talking about something else. You know how many people crying, "Lord have mercy"? I don't want to hear nothing about God. Billy Cisco crying, "Lord have mercy" and got hit by a truck. Myrtle Johnson. 1522 Stemrod Street down in Montgomery, Alabama. Had eight kids get burned up in a fire. Where was God at then?

STOOL PIGEON: Job said, "The Lord giveth and the Lord taketh away."

ELMORE: I don't want to hear nothing about Job. I'm talking about Myrtle Johnson. That's who I'm talking about.

STOOL PIGEON: "All the trials and tribulations that prevail against you shall come to naught for I shall be a protection and a fortress for thee."

ELMORE: Go tell that to Myrtle Johnson.

STOOL PIGEON: She know. God's a Great Comforter. There is a Balm in Gilead even though some people don't think so.

ELMORE: I don't want to hear that. God ain't got nothing to do with it.

KING: God's only in charge of some things.

ELMORE: You in charge. Who else gonna be in charge but you? It's your life. I'm sixty-six years old and I can do anything I want. I don't have to ask nobody nothing. If I can bear up under the consequences I can make a pit bull shit bricks and

don't have to tell nobody how or why I done it. 'Cause I'm
the boss.

KING: I set me out a little circle and anything come inside my
circle I say what happen and don't happen. God's in charge
of some things. If I jump up and shoot you I ain't gonna
blame it on God. That's where I'm the boss . . . I can decide
whether you live or die. I'm in charge of that.

ELMORE: Naw, naw, wait a minute . . . you ain't in charge of
whether I live or die.

KING: Who's in charge? It ain't God.

ELMORE: I'm in charge! I ain't gonna just let you up and kill me.
If it come to that it be me or you.

KING: See what I'm saying? That's the way it was with Pernell. It
was me or him. Only I was in charge. I was the boss that
day. And I'm in charge today.

ELMORE: Question: What if you in somebody else's circle and
you don't know it? And all the time you thinking you in
charge?

KING: They got a name for that.

MISTER: It's called a rude awakening.

ELMORE: The reason I ask is 'cause you all already in my circle.

KING: You might wake up and find out otherwise.

(*Tonya, obviously upset, enters from the street.*)

MISTER: Hey, Tonya.

(*Tonya ignores everyone and continues into the house.*)

She mad about something.

KING: Tonya . . . Tonya!

(*Tonya exits without answering. King follows her.*)

MISTER: I got to get to work. I'm gonna be late again. (*He exits*)

KING (*Offstage*): Tonya!

RUBY (*Offstage*): Leave her alone.

KING (*Offstage*): What's the matter?

TONYA (*Offstage*): You ain't got nothing to do with this.

(*Elmore exits into the house.*)

KING (*Offstage*): What's this? Where you been?

RUBY (*Offstage*): Leave her alone.

KING (*Offstage*): What I say don't count?

RUBY (*Offstage*): Leave her alone.

KING (*Offstage*): This my business, woman. Why don't you leave me go with my business. How many times I got to tell you.

(*Tonya enters the yard, starts to exit, changes her mind. King enters, looks at Tonya for a beat.*)

TONYA: You ain't got nothing to do with this. You don't even know nothing about it. What you know about having a baby?

KING: I know all I need to know. What else am I supposed to know? You the woman.

TONYA: I ain't having this baby. That's all there is to it.

KING: You had Natasha. What's the difference?

TONYA: About seventeen years. That's a whole lot of difference. I'm thirty-five years old. I done seen the whole thing turn around. When I had Natasha I was as happy as I could be. I had something nobody could take away from me. Had somebody to love. Had somebody to love me. I thought life was gonna be something. Look up and the whole world seem like it went crazy. Her daddy in jail. Her step-daddy going to jail. She seventeen and got a baby, she don't even know who the father is. She moving so fast she can't stop and look in the mirror. She can't see herself. All anybody got to do is look at her good and she run off and lay down with them. She don't think no further than that. Ain't got no future 'cause she don't know how to make one. Don't nobody care nothing about that. All they care about is getting a bigger TV. All she care about is the next time somebody gonna look at her and want to lay down with her.

KING: You wasn't too old to lay down yourself. You wasn't too old for that part.

TONYA: King, I don't want to go through it.

KING: What I say don't mean nothing. That's what you telling me?

TONYA: It ain't like it don't mean nothing, King. It don't mean everything like you think it ought to mean. There's other people in the world.

KING: Am I messing with them? I know there's other people in the world. I'm talking about my life.

TONYA: It's my life, too. That's what you don't see.

KING: Your life is my life. That's what you can't see. I'm living for you. That's what I told you when we got married. I love my Tonya. That's what I told the minister. I said, "My life is your life." Love got to mean something. If it don't mean that, what do it mean? Everything I do I do for you.

TONYA: It seem like you do it for Neesi.

KING: Neesi gone. That don't mean I got to forget her. I loved Neesi. I ain't never gonna love nobody like I loved Neesi. I told you that. That don't mean I don't love you. Neesi gone. You here. I got to go on with my life. But I ain't gonna forget Neesi. I can't do nothing for Neesi. I can't even pray for her. God turn the other way. He don't want to hear nothing from me. You trying to change the subject. I'm talking about that's my baby. Now you done went down to the place to get an abortion without telling me. You can't just go get rid of it.

TONYA: Why? Look at Natasha. I couldn't give her what she needed. Why I wanna go back and do it again? I ain't got nothing else to give. I can't give myself. How I'm gonna give her? I don't understand what to do . . . how to be a mother. You either love too much or don't love enough. Don't seem like there's no middle ground. I look up, she ten years old and I'm still trying to figure out life. Figure out what happened.

Next thing I know she grown. Talking about she a woman. Just 'cause you can lay down and open your legs to a man don't make you a woman. I tried to tell her that. She's a baby! She don't know nothing about life. What she know? Who taught her? I'm trying to figure it out myself. Time I catch up, it's moved on to something else. I got to watch her being thrown down a hole it's gonna take her a lifetime to crawl out and I can't do nothing to help her. I got to stand by and watch her. Why I wanna go back through all that? I don't want to have a baby that younger than my grandchild. Who turned the world around like that? What sense that make? I'm thirty-five years old. Don't seem like there's nothing left. I'm through with babies. I ain't raising no more. Ain't raising no grandkids. I'm looking out for Tonya. I ain't raising no kid to have somebody shoot him. To have his friends shoot him. To have the police shoot him. Why I want to bring another life into this world that don't respect life? I don't want to raise no more babies when you got to fight to keep them alive. You take Little Buddy Will's mother up on Bryn Mawr Road. What she got? A heartache that don't never go away. She up there now sitting down in her living room. She got to sit down 'cause she can't stand up. She sitting down trying to figure it out. Trying to figure out what happened. One minute her house is full of life. The next minute it's full of death. She was waiting for him to come home and they bring her a corpse. Say, "Come down and make the identification. Is this your son?" Got a tag on his toe say "John Doe." They got to put a number on it. John Doe number four. She got the dinner on the table. Say, "Junior like fried chicken." She got some of that. Say, "Junior like string beans." She got some of that. She don't know Junior ain't eating no more. He got a pile of clothes she washing up. She don't know Junior don't need no more clothes. She look in the closet. Junior ain't got no suit. She got to go buy him a suit. He can't try it on. She got to guess the size. Somebody come up and tell her, "Miss So-and-So, your boy got shot." She know before they say it.

Her knees start to get weak. She shaking her head. She don't want to hear it. Somebody call the police. They come and pick him up off the sidewalk. Dead nigger on Bryn Mawr Road. They got to quit playing cards and come and pick him up. They used to take pictures. They don't even take pictures no more. They pull him out of the freezer and she look at him. She don't want to look. They make her look. What to do now? The only thing to do is call the undertaker. The line is busy. She got to call back five times. The undertaker got so much business he don't know what to do. He losing sleep. He got to hire two more helpers to go with the two he already got. He don't even look at the bodies no more. He couldn't tell you what they look like. He only remember the problems he have with them. This one so big and fat if he fall off the table it take six men to pick him up. That one ain't got no cheek. That one eyes won't stay closed. The other one been dead so long he got maggots coming out his nose. The family can't pay for that one. The coroner wants to see the other one again. That one's mother won't go home. The other one . . . (*She stops to catch her breath*) I ain't going through that. I ain't having this baby . . . and I ain't got to explain it to nobody. (*She starts to exits into the house*)

KING (*Calling after her*): You got to explain it to me! You just can't go get rid of it. I don't care if you do have to call the undertaker. That's life, woman! Can't nobody say what's gonna happen. It ain't even born and you got it in a casket already.

(*Tonya exits into the house.*)

You got things backwards. Talking about you ain't got to explain it to nobody. (*He goes to the door of the house and yells inside*) You got to explain it to me!

(*Ruby enters from the house.*)

RUBY: King.

40

KING: Leave me go with my business, woman.

RUBY: You keep pushing Tonya away and she's gonna stay away.

KING: I don't need you to tell me nothing. Go tell her. She the one got it backwards.

RUBY: It ain't gonna take you no time to be sorry. It's gonna come up on you quick. I done seen it happen. You're gonna look up one day and find yourself all alone.

KING: Go on now and leave go with my business. I don't need you to tell me nothing. Go tell Walter Kelly.

(King exits the yard. Tonya enters from the house.)

TONYA: Where's King?

RUBY: He's gone off somewhere.

TONYA: King thinks it all about him. He thinks he's the only one in the world. I done told him I ain't having this baby. He act like he got something to do with it.

RUBY: I done tried everything I know. King don't believe I love him. It's a mother's love. It don't never go away. I love me but I love King more. Sometimes I might not love me but there don't never come a time I don't love him. He don't understand that.

TONYA: He understand. He just stubborn.

RUBY: King don't know he lucky to be here. I didn't want to have no baby. Seem to me like I got off to a bad start. I wanted to have an abortion. Somebody sent me up there to see Aunt Ester. I thought she did abortions. It didn't take me long to find out I was in the wrong place. She was sitting in a room with a red curtain. A little old woman wearing a stocking cap. I can't say if she had any teeth or not. She was just sitting there. Told me to come closer where she could put her hands on my head. I got real peaceful. Seem like all my problems went away. She told me man can plant the seed but only God can make it grow. Told me God was a good judge. I told her that's what scared me. She just laughed and told me, "God has three hands. Two for that baby and one for the rest of us." That's just the way she said it. "God got three hands. Two for that baby and one for the rest of us. You got your time coming." I never will forget that. I used to look at King and try and figure it out. But I ain't seen nothing to make her say that. I thought maybe she was just telling me that but she ain't supposed to lie about nothing like that. I just ain't never seen nothing that would make him that special. That's what I'm telling you about that baby you carrying. You never know what God have planned. You can't all the time see it. That's what Louise used to tell me. You can't all the time see it but God can see it good.

TONYA: I wish he'd tell me what he got planned. It look like everything going every which way and ain't nobody in charge. You got all these kids . . . don't look like there's nothing for them. Wasn't nothing for me and now ain't nothing for them. Natasha just like I was. Seem like something should have changed.

RUBY: Life's got its own rhythm. It don't always go along with your rhythm. It don't always be what you think it's gonna be.

ELMORE (*From inside the house*): Ruby! You got this chicken burning up in here.

RUBY (*Starting to exit into the house*): That's all life is . . . trying to match up them two rhythms. You ever match them up and you won't have to worry about nothing. (*She exits into the house*)

(*The lights go down on the scene.*)

SCENE 3

The lights come up on Elmore sitting on the steps cleaning his pistol. It is the next morning. Ruby enters from the house.

RUBY: I'm gonna put on a pot of grits and fry some bacon and eggs. (*She notices the gun*) Why don't you put that gun up? You know I don't like to see it.

(Elmore puts the gun back into his pocket.)

ELMORE: You remember Stoller, don't you? Old big fat Stoller? He died about two years ago. The undertaker had to wait two weeks to get him a big enough casket. He had to send all the way to New York. Stoller died of a heart attack. He was walking down the street and died in the middle of the block. He was trying to go to the bar on the corner and never got there.

RUBY: He had about three different wives. He so fat I don't know why any woman would want him.

ELMORE: He keep money. I ain't never know him not to have money. He would have money when I didn't. The women like that. Of course, now with me . . . they like me for something else. Ain't that right?

RUBY: You wasn't such hot stuff.

ELMORE: Not with you. You was the fire. The best thing you could do with you was try and not get burned up. You couldn't try and put the fire out. That's why I had to get away. I see where I was starting to get trapped in a burning room.

RUBY: You got away 'cause you wanted to.

ELMORE: I wanted to be by myself. I hadn't taken the time to stop and find out what a woman was. Then when I met you . . . you just confused me. I told myself I wanted to be by myself for a while so I could figure it out. I always figured I was gonna come back for you. Then that thing with Leroy happened and you got away from me. But I never did stop loving you. My love for you is strong. It must be. I been carrying it going on thirty-seven years now. I can't even remember a time I didn't know your name. I done loved a thousand women in my life but you can't turn my love for you around. I done tried. Every time I try to get it off me it come back stronger. That's why I'm here. I can't do without you.

RUBY: They done run you out of somewhere. That's why you here. You ain't got nowhere else to be.

ELMORE: I told you I'm going down to Cleveland. I got some business down there. After I take care of my business I'm coming back.

RUBY: It's time to slow down. You done seen everything what's out there. You done been all over the map. What else is there for you?

ELMORE: Life got all kinds of things. You can't predict life. Hell, I might get lucky and find me a million dollars laying on the sidewalk. That make up for the million I done spent.

RUBY: You never did find her, did you?

ELMORE: Who? Find who?

RUBY: Whoever you was looking for. Seem like nothing was enough for you. Seem like you wanted to have everything at the same time. Life don't work like that.

ELMORE: I wanted to have it to where I could get a handle on it. Only that was a large sucker to try and wrestle to the ground. It took me a long time to figure out I didn't have to do that. I could just learn to live with life.

RUBY: Leroy didn't want everything. He was satisfied with what he had.

ELMORE: Come on now . . . we was having a nice time.

RUBY: That's the only man ever treated me right.

ELMORE: Come on now.

RUBY: He dead and gone now. I used to feel guilty about loving you but I got over that. I seen where it wasn't my fault. Wasn't nothing I could do. You ain't got no say over who you love. You ain't got to follow up on it but you ain't got no say over that. Life say. Sometime it say wrong but you still got to carry that love whether it's right or wrong. Many a time I wanted to kill you. Get that guilt off me.

ELMORE: If you wanna kill me you better hurry up. The doctor say this thing is killing me by degrees and ain't but so many degrees left. I'm dying on my feet.

RUBY: Elmore!

ELMORE: You gonna be here till you gone. We all got to go that way. You know that from the beginning.

(There is a long pause.)

You never did tell King that Leroy was his daddy, did you?

RUBY: He don't need to know that. What he need to know that for? He thinks Hedley was his father. He don't need to know no different.

ELMORE: Then you better hope he never sees a picture of Leroy. He looks just like him.

RUBY: You better hope he never find out. He's liable to kill you if he finds out.

ELMORE: Me and Leroy was man-to-man.

RUBY: That don't mean nothing. What that mean?

ELMORE: He ought to be able to understand that.

RUBY: King only understand what he wants to. He like you when it comes to that.

ELMORE: I understand what I need to. I got good understanding. That's what I told the doctor. I believe King got good understanding too. King a man. Men know what other men know. I'm gonna tell him.

RUBY: You better not tell him. It ain't your place to tell him.

ELMORE: I need to tell him. I ain't gonna carry this to my grave. I made my peace with God but I got to make peace with myself. I'm gonna find out what kind of man he is.

RUBY: You ain't gonna mess this up like you mess up everything.

ELMORE: I need to tell him.

RUBY: I never should have listened to you telling me to send him to Louise. Talking about we could get married. What did that lead to? It don't never lead to nothing but trouble with you. Talking about we could get married and I could get King back. And then you walked out. You walked out 'cause you was scared. I woke up and went looking for you. I thought you was on the couch. Then I saw where the door was open. I looked all around and you was gone. I had to go see the doctor, I felt so bad.

ELMORE: I went down to Kansas City to get some money. You can't get married without no money.

RUBY: The doctor told me there wasn't nothing he could do.

ELMORE: I come back and you was gone.

RUBY: I told myself after that there wasn't nothing for me. I may as well crawl in a hole. I didn't think I was gonna last.

ELMORE: You should have had faith in me. If you had faith in me, we would have had the world on a silver platter.

RUBY: You just used that as an excuse to walk out.

ELMORE: I went down to Kansas City to get some money to come back and get you.

RUBY: I wasn't waiting on you.

ELMORE: I come on back through and you was gone.

RUBY: Wasn't nothing there for me. I went home and buried my mama and went on up to Philadelphia.

ELMORE: I heard about your mother dying.

RUBY: Wasn't nothing in Philadelphia either. Then I found out King was in jail. Louise had leukemia and I asked myself what more is there. It couldn't get no worse. I was all right after that. Everything smoothed out. I quit worrying about life. I seen what it was gonna be. Why'd you leave me?

ELMORE: You was hard to take. I seen where I wasn't gonna do nothing but fight with you. As long as you was singing you was all right. When you wasn't singing you was hard to take.

RUBY: I quit singing. I give it up. You was supposed to be there. I always felt that. I got to have somebody too. I saw you and said you was supposed to be mine. I turned around and you come out the club. Had your hands in your pocket. I never will forget seeing you standing there. Had on that hat. I remember you asked me my name. I was glad you said something to me.

ELMORE: I couldn't take my eyes off your mouth. The way you said your name told me you was all the woman you wanted to be. I hadn't seen that in a woman before.

RUBY: You used to tell me I was pretty.

ELMORE: You still pretty. You just got old. We both got old.

(There is a long silence.)

Let's get married.

RUBY: I ain't going back through that. I'm too old. The time to get married was back when. You wait till you dying, then you want to talk about getting married.

ELMORE: It ain't never too late.

RUBY: It's too late for me. I don't wanna be a wife one day and a widow the next. All I'm looking to do is get in one of these senior-citizen high-rise and enjoy whatever little bit of time I got left. You talk about getting married and the next thing you know you out the door.

ELMORE: I told you I'm a new man.

RUBY: That's what you talk ... you a new man. You can talk anything. I ain't gonna fall for all this new man talk. I'm a new woman.

ELMORE: I got to go to Cleveland but I'm coming back. Then we can get married. I'm gonna show you I done changed and I can't be without you.

RUBY: Where my present? You said you brought me a present.

ELMORE: I got it in my suitcase. You gonna like it.

(Elmore exits into the house. Ruby goes over and looks at seeds. Mister enters.)

MISTER: How you doing, Miss Ruby? Where King, he in the house?

RUBY: He gone out to Sears to pick up Tonya's pictures. He been gone a while, he should be back.

MISTER: I was on my way to work. I just stopped by.

RUBY: Where you working? I need me a job.

MISTER: I work making nails. Right down there on Penn Avenue. We got a little place where we make nails.

RUBY: I don't know how to make no nails. The only kind of work I know how to do is singing.

MISTER: I been down there about nine months. If I don't get a raise soon I'm gonna quit. I'm supposed to get a raise after six months.

RUBY: I know how to press shirts on the machine. But mostly I just worked at singing. That's the only kind of work I know to do. I used to sing with a band. A man named Walter Kelly. That was back in East St. Louis. A long time ago.

MISTER: My daddy played drums. That's the only one I know in the music business.

RUBY: I knew Red Carter. I knew your daddy. That's how I got to East St. Louis. He introduced me to Walter Kelly when he was putting his band together. He wanted your daddy to play drums but he never did. I don't know why.

(Ruby sings. She sings badly but it is obvious she knows her way around a song; her voice is just shot:)

Red sails in the sunset
Way out to sea
Oh carry my loved one
Bring him home safely to me.

MISTER: That sound like one of them old songs Ella Fitzgerald or Sarah Vaughn used to sing.

RUBY: That was King's favorite song. He used to walk around saying, "Sing 'Red Sails,' Mommy. Sing 'Red Sails.'" I always thought I was gonna make a record but when the time come Walter Kelly got somebody else. Walter Kelly was a big man. We had a falling-out one time. We sorta made up but it never was the same.

MISTER: It be that way with most people. But you never can forget it. What they done wrong just sticks with you. That's the way it was with me and my daddy. He was supposed to take me with him to Alabama one time. To see my grandmother. Had my suitcase packed and everything. He met some woman the night before we was to leave. He left me and took her instead. It was never right between me and him after that. Woman named Edna Stewart. Lived right across the street from the funeral home and didn't even come to his funeral. *(Pause)* You should go down to Crawford Grill when they got the band down there. If you ask them I bet they'd let you sing. I don't know if they gonna pay you though.

RUBY: I don't sing no more, I quit singing. The people used to like it when I sang. They'd clap and some of them would holler. They'd tell me afterward that I sang real nice. Then I'd go home and lay down and cry 'cause it was so lonely. I thought singing was supposed to be something special.

(Elmore enters from the house.)

MISTER: Hey, Elmore.
ELMORE: How you doing?
MISTER: I don't know. It's too early to tell.

(Elmore hands Ruby a jewelry box.)

ELMORE: I got this in New York.

(Ruby opens the box. There is a necklace inside. It is cheap costume jewelry.)

RUBY: Look at this!
ELMORE: That's real gold. Twenty-four karat gold. Cost me four hundred dollars. Go on. Put it on. Here, let me help you.
RUBY: It's got little diamonds.
ELMORE: That's gold and silver.

(Elmore helps Ruby put the necklace on.)

RUBY: I need me a dress to wear with it.
ELMORE: You can get you a dress. You can go down and pick it out.

MISTER: That look real nice, Miss Ruby. Like you a queen or something.

RUBY: Let me go put on these grits. *(She exits into the house)*

MISTER: I got to get on to work before I get fired.

ELMORE: How much money you got?

MISTER: My mama told me not to tell nobody. She say, "Do Gimbels tell Kaufmann's their business?"

ELMORE: If you got enough money I'll be able to do something nice for you. *(With a flourish, he hands Mister a derringer)* Look at that. You didn't even see me give it to you.

MISTER: This a derringer. Where you get this from?

ELMORE: Most people ain't never seen a derringer. They know what it is but they ain't never seen none.

MISTER: I always said I was gonna get one of these. Seem like it be easy to hide.

ELMORE: You can hide it right in your hand. *(He demonstrates)* That way you be ready when you have to. You never know with these young punks running around these days.

MISTER: This is real nice.

ELMORE: How much money you got?

MISTER: I got fifty dollars.

ELMORE: Give me seventy-five dollars. I even got three bullets.

MISTER: I ain't got but fifty dollars.

ELMORE: Cost you seventy-five dollars. Look, it's got a pearl handle. That's what you call mother-of-pearl. That's better than pearl. Got a nicer shine. That's why they call it mother-of-pearl. I need some money, otherwise I'd hold on to it.

MISTER: I ain't got no seventy-five dollars. They supposed to give me a raise. If this be next month or something I might have it. I ain't got but fifty dollars.

ELMORE: I need to get seventy-five. I may as well hold on to it for fifty.

MISTER: I might be able to throw in another five dollars.

ELMORE: Okay, make it ten. Throw another five on top of that.

MISTER: I just got the fifty-five dollars. That's scraping the bottom of the barrel. If I give you that I got to figure out how

I'm gonna eat and get my clothes out the cleaners. Come to think about it . . . you might have to wait till I get paid before I can spend anything.

ELMORE: Give me the fifty-five dollars.

MISTER: Do it work?

ELMORE: Yeah it work. You don't think I be selling you a gun that don't work, do you? You subject to get mad and go get one that do. Now if I try and sell you a watch, you better watch out. Let the buyer beware.

MISTER: Give me one of them bullets and let me see if it work.

(Mister puts a bullet in the gun, aims at the ground and pulls the trigger. It doesn't fire. Elmore takes the gun from him.)

ELMORE: You got to cock back the hammer first.

(Elmore cocks back the hammer and fires the gun. It misfires. He bangs it with his hand and cocks back the hammer again. It fires. Ruby comes to the door.)

RUBY: What you all doing out there?

ELMORE: We ain't doing nothing. *(To Mister)* Go on and give me sixty dollars.

MISTER: Naw, you said fifty-five. That's all I got.

ELMORE: All right, give me that.

(Mister gives Elmore the money and puts the derringer in his pocket.)

Don't tell nobody where you got it from. *(To Ruby)* We ain't doing nothing. How them grits coming?

RUBY: They almost done.

ELMORE: Well, where the biscuits? I know you got some biscuits. Go on back in the house and make some biscuits.

RUBY: You gonna look up, find yourself eating these grits out there in the alley. *(She exits into the house)*

ELMORE: You got some bullets. I got two bullets. I'll let you have them for five dollars. They special bullets.

MISTER: Naw . . . naw . . . you said . . .

ELMORE: I ain't said they come with it. I said I had them. It cost you five dollars if you want the bullets. A gun ain't worth nothing without the bullets.

(Mister gives him the five dollars.)

MISTER: All right. I'm gonna remember that.

(King enters. He is mad.)

ELMORE: Hey, King.

KING: They ain't got the pictures.

MISTER: What pictures?

KING: Tonya's pictures. They ain't got the pictures. Told me they can't find them and they ain't got no record of them. I showed him the receipt and he told me that didn't count. I started to grab him by his throat. How in the hell the receipt not gonna count? That's like money. I told his dumb ass to get the manager. The manager come talking about their system. Say it's based on phone numbers. I told him I didn't care about his system. A receipt is a receipt all over the world. You can't have no system where a receipt don't count. You can't just go making up the rules. I don't care if you Sears and Roebuck, Kmart or anybody else. You can't make up no rule where a receipt don't count. I tried to tell him this politely like Mama Louise taught me. He wasn't listening. He trying to talk while I'm talking. I told him, "Motherfucker, shut up and listen to me!" He threatened to call the police. I told him he better call the United States Marines too. The police come and threatened to arrest me. They tried to take my receipt. I told them they have to kill me first. Without that receipt I'm going to jail. They gonna charge me with fraud, forgery, extortion, grand theft,

larceny, second-degree robbery and anything else they can
think of. They took the number off the receipt and said they
would track the pictures down.

MISTER: They should have did that in the first place.

KING: They so busy talking about their system they got to prove
to me the receipt don't count. See, they don't know but they
gonna give me my goddamn pictures, I don't bother nobody.
But I can turn that around real quick.

ELMORE: Give them a chance to look it up . . . they'll find them.
Sometime you play the jack when you should have played
the ace. But that don't mean the queen is bad luck. Give
them a chance they'll find them.

KING: Naw, you don't understand, Elmore.

ELMORE: I understand. The motherfuckers got your pictures
and can't find them.

KING: Naw, that ain't what the problem is. Ask Mister. The
problem is they tell me my receipt don't count. That's what
the problem is. They don't tell you it don't count when they
give it to you. They even tell you, "Don't forget your receipt."
Then they gonna tell you it don't count.

MISTER: It count for everybody else. Why all of a sudden it
don't count when it's you?

KING: You see what I'm saying. That's like telling me I don't
count.

MISTER: They got different rules for different people.

ELMORE: Boy, you wouldn't have lasted three days in Alabama
in 1948. I done got my ass whipped so many times I done lost
count. That taught me a lot of things. You like I used to be.
You gonna fight all that battles. You don't know you don't
have to do that. You got to pick and choose when to fight. If
you pick and choose the right place you'll always be victori-
ous. The way you going, they gonna give you a free ride to
the county jail. Six months later when you get out, your pictures gonna be sitting right there waiting on you.

KING: They ought to be waiting on me now. They got everything
stacked up against you as it is. Every time I try to do some-

thing they get in the way. It's been that way my whole life. Every time I try to do something they get in the way. Especially if you try and get some money. They don't want you to have none of that. They keep that away from you. They got fifty-eleven way to get money and don't want you to have none. They block you at every turn. Hop been tearing down buildings his whole life and all of a sudden he don't know what he doing. He don't know how to tear down buildings. They can't give him the contract. They afraid he gonna make a little bit of money. But you ask Mister . . . I ain't gonna be poor all my life. I ain't gonna die a poor man.

MISTER: The white man got fifty-eleven way to get money and go to school to learn some more ways. If you go to one of them schools, say, "I'm gonna learn how to make money" . . . they'll give you a mop and bucket. Say, "You be the janitor."

KING: That's what my fifth-grade teacher told me.

MISTER: "You be the janitor. I'm gonna stand over here and smoke cigars." They don't know . . . I can smoke cigars too.

KING: My fifth-grade teacher told me I was gonna make a good janitor. Say she can tell that by how good I erased the blackboards. Had me believing it. I come home and told Mama Louise I wanted to be a janitor. She told me I could be anything I wanted. I say, "Okay, I'll be a janitor." I thought that was what I was supposed to be. I didn't know no better. That was the first job I got. Cleaning up that bar used to be down on Wylie. Got one job the man told me he was gonna shoot me if he caught me stealing anything. I ain't worked for him ten minutes. I quit right there. He calling me a thief before I start. Neesi told me I shouldn't have quit. But I'm a man. I don't bother nobody. And I know right from wrong. I know what's right for me. That's where me and the rest of the people part ways. Tonya ask me say, "When we gonna move?" She want a decent house. One the plaster ain't falling off the walls. I say, "Okay but I got to wait." What I'm waiting on? I don't know. I'm just waiting. I told myself I'm waiting for things to change. That mean I'm gonna be living here forever.

Tonya deserve better than that. I go for a job and they say, "What can you do." I say, "I can do anything. If you give me the tanks and the airplanes I can go out there and win any war that's out there."

MISTER: If you had the tanks, the airplanes and the boats . . . you could conquer the world.

KING: I can dance all night if the music's right. Ain't nothing I can't do. I could build a railroad if I had the steel and a gang of men to drive the spikes. I ain't limited to nothing. I can go down there and do Mellon's job. I know how to count money. I don't loan money to everybody who ask me. I know how to do business. I'm talking about mayor . . . governor, I can do it all. I ain't got no limits. I know right from wrong. I know which way the wind blow too. It don't blow my way. Mellon got six houses. I ain't got none. But that don't mean he six times a better man than me.

MISTER: That just mean the wind blow his way.

KING: I got to make it whatever way I can. I got to try and make it blow some over here. I don't want much. Just a little bit. Why you got to have it all. Give me some. I ain't bothering nobody. I got to feel right about myself. I look around and say, "Where the barbed wire?" They got everything else. They got me blocked in every other way. "Where the barbed wire?"

MISTER: If they had some barbed wire you could cut through it. But you can't cut through not having no job. You can't cut through that. That's better than barbed wire.

KING: You try and tell these niggers that and they look at you like you crazy. It was all right when they ain't had to pay you. They had plenty of work for you back then. Now that they got to pay you there ain't no work for you. I used to be worth twelve hundred dollars during slavery. Now I'm worth $3.35 an hour. I'm going backwards. Everybody else moving forward.

MISTER: The lady that own the store got her a bigger store to go with her bigger house. If she could drive she'd have a bigger car.

KING: Everybody moving forward. I went backward to $3.35 an hour.

MISTER: Sometime you quit your job thinking you can get another one. Nine months later you still be broke and then you be sorry.

KING: I ain't sorry for nothing I done. And ain't gonna be sorry. I'm gonna see to that. 'Cause I'm gonna do the right thing. Always. It ain't in me to do nothing else. We might disagree about what that is. But I know what is right for me. As long as I draw a breath in my body I'm gonna do the right thing for me. What I got to be sorry for? People say, "Ain't you sorry you killed Pernell?" I ain't sorry I killed Pernell. The nigger deserve to die. He cut my face. I told the judge, "Not guilty." They thought I was joking. I say, "The motherfucker cut me! How can I be wrong for killing him?" That's common sense. I don't care what the law say. The law don't understand this. It must not. They wanna take and lock me up. Where's the understanding? If a burglar break in a white man's house to steal his TV and the white man shoot him they don't say he wrong. The law understand that. They pat him on the back and tell him to go on home.

MISTER: How's stealing somebody's TV gonna be worse than somebody cutting your face open?

KING: You see what I'm saying? The jury come back and say, "Guilty." They asked them one by one. They all said, "Guilty." Had nine white men and three white women. They all said, "Guilty." They wouldn't look at me. I told them to look at me. Look at that scar.

MISTER: It ain't like Pernell was sitting at home eating dinner when he was killed.

KING: Had a nine-millimeter, two knives . . .

MISTER: . . . and a razor!

KING: I got closer to where they could see my scar. The judge like to had a fit. They had six deputies come at me from all sides. They said I tried to attack the jury. I was just trying to get closer so they could see my face. They tried to run out the door. They took and put me in solitary confinement. Said I was unruly.

MISTER: They put that on you in third grade when you kicked Miss Biggs.

KING: You remember that? I had to go to the bathroom. Teacher say, "You got to do number one or number two?" Now, what kind of sense is that? What she care?

MISTER: Why she got to know?

KING: I looked at her like she was crazy. Why somebody want to know that? I must have been taking too long to answer and she told me to sit back down. Mama Louise always told me don't be no fool, so I guess the time had come to see how smart I was. I could either sit back down and pee in my pants or I could walk out the door and go down the hall to the bathroom. I started to walk out the door and she grabbed me and I kicked her. They said I was unruly. That stuck with me all the way through the twelfth grade. I went to school every day and didn't learn nothing. I got a high school diploma. What that mean? That don't mean people treat you any better.

MISTER: They still treat you like you're a seventh-grade dropout.

KING: But I got honor and dignity even though some people don't think that. I was born with it. Mama Louise told me don't let nobody take it from me.

ELMORE: The way you keep your dignity is to make your own rules. If you want to beat the system you got to step outside of it. You got to make your own rules. You ain't doing nothing but breaking their rules. That's what the problem is. They hustling you and you don't know it. See, if I break a rule it be my rule. That's the only rules I can break . . . 'cause that's the only ones I live by. *(He steps on the seeds)*

KING: Hey, Elmore! What you doing? Stepping on my seeds! See! That's what I'm talking about! Everybody always fucking with me. Why you wanna step on my seeds?

ELMORE: I ain't seen them there. How the hell I'm supposed to know there was seeds there.

(King gets on his knees and smoothes over the ground.)

KING: Open your eyes and look. That's what's wrong with niggers now. They can't see past their nose. Look at that! They were growing. Everybody telling me I need some good dirt!

(Stool Pigeon enters from his house.)

This is good dirt! Look at that! This is good dirt! A seed supposed to grow in dirt! Look at this. Look at that dirt! That's good dirt. They were growing and you stepped on them! This is good dirt! It is! Look! Look! This is good dirt! It's good dirt! Everybody better back the fuck up off me! See . . . 'cause people don't know. I got some announcements to make too. That's why I killed Pernell. If you get to the bottom line . . . I want everybody to know that King Hedley II is here. And I want everybody to know, just like my daddy, that you can't fuck with me. I want you to get the picture. Each and every one of you! And I want you to hold me to it. When you see me coming, that's who you better see. Now they done had World War I . . . and World War II . . . the next motherfucker that fucks with me it's gonna be World War III.

(The lights go down on the scene.)

Act Two

Scene I

The lights come up on the yard. Stool Pigeon enters carrying a dead black cat. He has dug a hole near King's plot of seeds and begins to bury the cat. Tonya enters from the house.

TONYA: Stool Pigeon, what you doing? What you got there?

STOOL PIGEON: The cat laying out there on the sidewalk. Deader than a doornail. I thought a dog might have got it but it ain't got a scratch on it.

TONYA: Maybe somebody poisoned him.

STOOL PIGEON: Her! Poisoned her! This a female cat. She ain't been poisoned. You'd be able to tell.

TONYA: What you doing?

STOOL PIGEON: What it look like I'm doing? (*He lays the cat down in the grave*)

TONYA: I know you ain't burying that cat out here. Ruby gonna have a fit. If she even think of that cat buried out here she gonna have a fit. You should have called the city. They'll come out and get it.

STOOL PIGEON: This ain't the city's cat. This a black cat. I'm gonna take some of the bark off that tree and put that on there. You sprinkle some blood on there and she coming back in seven days if she ain't used up her nine lives. I was gonna put some pigeon blood on there but that ain't gonna work. God want your best. If I knew where to get a goat I'd kill him and spill his blood on there. That might work. Either that or a fatted calf.

TONYA: I don't believe in all that stuff. You go crazy trying to keep up with all that stuff. Why you believe in that?

STOOL PIGEON: You ain't got to believe in it for it to be true. Where's King?

TONYA: He went out to Homewood. (*She walks over and looks at the grave*) Why you bury that cat here?

STOOL PIGEON: The city charge ten dollars to pick up a dead cat.

TONYA: Not if they don't know whose it is.

STOOL PIGEON: This Aunt Ester's cat. If I tell the city I don't know whose cat this is I'll never be able to sleep through the night again. Where's King?

TONYA: I told you he went out to Homewood. He'll be back soon. What you want to see him for?

STOOL PIGEON: I got something for him.

TONYA: Wait till Ruby find out about that cat.

STOOL PIGEON: King want to be like the eagle. He want to go to the top of the mountain. He wanna sit on top of the world. Only he ain't got no wings. He got to climb up. He don't know you need the Key to the mountain. The mountain ain't for everybody. God don't give everybody the same. King don't know God got a hand in it. It's His creation. King get a Key to the mountain and he'll be all right. Only he don't know he looking for it. He liable to walk right by it.

(*King enters carrying a roll of barbed wire. He goes to his plot of dirt where the seeds are, notices the cat's grave and stops.*)

KING: What's that there?

STOOL PIGEON: Aunt Ester's cat died. I buried it over there.

KING: Don't mess with my seeds. (*He draws a line with his foot*)

STOOL PIGEON: If she ain't used up her nine lives Aunt Ester coming back.

KING: Just don't mess with my seeds.

(*King begins to build a barrier around his seeds with the barbed wire. Stool Pigeon watches him.*)

STOOL PIGEON: They got razor wire now. That barbed wire ain't good enough no more.

KING: It's good enough for me. (*Stool Pigeon exits into his house. King looks at Tonya*) Go on in the house and leave me alone.

TONYA: I ain't bothering you.

KING: I said go on now. I don't want to be bothered.

(*Ruby enters.*)

RUBY: What you doing?

KING: I definitely don't want to be bothered with you. This is my business.

TONYA: Leave him alone, Miss Ruby. He just looking for something to get him started.

(*Ruby and Tonya exit into the house. Stool Pigeon enters with a machete wrapped in burlap; he sits on the steps and watches King for a moment.*)

KING: What you got there?

STOOL PIGEON: This the machete Hedley used to kill Floyd Barton. This is the machete of the Conquering Lion of Judea.

KING: Where you get that from?

STOOL PIGEON: Louise give it to me. The police give it back to her and she wanted to get it out of the house. I say, "I'm gonna keep it." I didn't know why. But now I know. This is yours. (*He gives King the machete*) I miss Floyd. It was a long time before I could forgive Hedley for something like that.

KING: Floyd shouldn't have tried to take my daddy's money.

STOOL PIGEON: It wasn't Hedley's money. Floyd stole that money. Him and a fellow named Poochie Tillery. Poochie got killed in the robbery and Floyd buried the money in the yard. I know 'cause I found it. I give it back to him 'cause it had blood on it.

KING: Floyd didn't try to take Hedley's money?

STOOL PIGEON: Hedley ain't had no money. He was waiting for the ghost of Buddy Bolden to bring him some. Say his father was gonna send it to him. After Floyd was killed Hedley showed me the money. Told me Buddy Bolden gave it to him. That's when I knew. I say, "I got to tell." What else could I do? Ruby called me "Stool Pigeon" and somehow or another it stuck. I'll tell anybody I'm a Truth Sayer. I think about Floyd sometimes but I know he in heaven. I saw him go up into heaven carried by angels dressed in black with black hats. Hedley saw them too. Him and Vera both. Time Foster laid his body in the ground, they opened the casket and snatched him straight up into the sky. I give that machete to you, and me and Hedley come full circle. That's yours. You can do with it what you want. If you find a way to wash that blood off you can go sit on top of the mountain. You be on top of the world. The Bible say, "Let him who knoweth duty redeem the house of his fathers from its iniquities against the Lord. And if he raise a cry and say he knoweth not the sins of his fathers then he knoweth not duty for even if the iniquities are great and his father's house be scattered to the numberless winds, if he shall gather it and raise it up then shall it stand even unto the end of time." Floyd was my friend. I give that to you and we can close the book on that chapter. I forgive. That's the Key to the mountain. God taught me how to do that. God can teach you a lot of things. He don't give you nothing you can't handle. God's a bad motherfucker!

(His duty done, Stool Pigeon exits into his house. King unwraps the machete. It is rusty. Mister enters.)

MISTER: Hey, King. What you got there? What's that?
KING: This was my father's machete. Stool Pigeon give it to me. Say this the machete that killed Floyd Barton. This the machete of the Conquering Lion of Judea. This is mine.
MISTER: Let me see it.

(King hands Mister the machete. Mister swings it around.)

I can see how you could kill somebody with this. If it was sharp. You need to sharpen it up. Put you some Rustoleum on there and that'll take all that rust off. Make it like new.
KING: I'm gonna take it to that meat market down on Fifth Avenue and get it sharpened.

(Mister hands the machete back to King; King wraps it up.)

MISTER: What you gonna do with it?
KING: I don't know. Stool Pigeon say he just give it to me. He don't know what I'm supposed to do with it either. I'm gonna take it out to Sears with me. I want to see them talk about their system then.

(Mister notices the barbed wire.)

MISTER: That's a good idea. I bet nobody won't step on there now. *(He notices the grave)* What's this?
KING: That cat died. Stool Pigeon buried her there.
MISTER: What cat?
KING: That cat was watching the hole. Aunt Ester's cat. She died.
MISTER: I was wondering why I ain't seen her up there. I thought she might have caught that rat and went on home. Come to find out she dead.

(Mister takes off his hat. King pulls a knit ski mask out of his pocket and puts it on.)

KING: I got these masks. How this look?

MISTER: That'll work. I can't tell who you are. You look like the Dark Avenger or somebody.

KING: I am.

(Mister pulls a pillowcase out of his bag.)

MISTER: I got this here. That's about the only thing Deanna left me. I ain't even got a pillow.

KING: You ain't got no pillow? I'll give you a pillow. You supposed to have a pillow. Where you sleeping at?

MISTER: On the floor. I got an old mattress I put down there.

KING: See, you should have treated her right. I told you she was gonna leave you. I could see it coming.

MISTER: I could see it coming too. But what I didn't see was she was gonna take all the furniture. Hey King, look here.

KING: What? What's that you got in your hand?

MISTER: Damn! You wasn't supposed to see it.

KING: What's that?

MISTER: This a derringer Elmore sold me.

KING: Let me see it.

(Mister hands King the derringer.)

MISTER: That's worth five hundred dollars.

KING: This ain't worth no five hundred dollars.

MISTER: That's silver. That's not just silver color. That's silver. And it's got a mother-of-pearl handle. That better than pearl. You can get five hundred dollars for that.

(King hands the derringer back to Mister.)

KING: Do it work?

mister: Yeah, it work. I'm gonna get me some silver bullets. Be like the Lone Ranger.

king: I ain't thinking about no Lone Ranger. (*He checks the clip*)

mister: That Glock is nice but a Beretta be better.

king: What you think? He keep the money under the counter.

mister: I don't think. I know. He keep it under the counter. Every time somebody buy something he put it in the cash register but then he take it out and put it under the counter. I seen him.

king: They got them two streets there.

mister: It got a door on the side. It lock from the inside. You can get out but you can't get in. You got to go around to the front to get in.

king: He got an alarm. It might be wired to the police station. I don't know.

mister: They got to take the time to get there. You take the same time to get away. That way you always be ahead of them. They got to come while you going.

king: What about the safe? He got a safe?

mister: I don't want to fool around with the safe. He keep most of the money under the counter. We get that and we be in and out of there in two minutes.

king: Don't nobody ever be in the back?

mister: Ain't got no back. Just got a little shelf where he work at. Off to the side. Kinda like behind the counter. I'll open that side door while you get the money. We can go out there and right up the alley. That way won't nobody see us. Only thing, don't take no jewelry. That's how you get caught. Trying to sell the jewelry. We don't want nothing but the money under the counter.

king: What you think be the best time?

mister: Right now. While it's quiet. Everybody done had their lunch and they be sleeping. Or else they be working. Now's the best time.

king: You all set?

mister: Yeah, I'm ready.

KING: You all right.
MISTER: Yeah.
KING: Let's go.

(*King grabs Mister.*)

I'm coming back. I ain't gonna be like Putter.
MISTER: Putter stopped to pick up the money. If you drop the money, just keep going.
KING: I ain't going back to jail either. You understand? I'm coming back.
MISTER: I got your back. I always got your back.
KING: I ain't gonna let nothing happen to you. We both coming back.
MISTER: Yeah.

(*They look at each other a long while.*)

KING: Come on. Let's go!

(*King and Mister exit the yard with a swagger—men with a dangerous job to do. The lights go down on the scene.*)

SCENE 2

The lights come up on the yard. King and Mister come running into the yard. King has the pillowcase under his coat. They stop and catch their breath.

MISTER: What was you doing! You gonna get us caught! I told you we don't want nothing but the money under the counter. You trying to get him to open up the safe.
KING: That's where the money at! What I'm there for but to get the money?
MISTER: I told you he keep the money under the counter.

KING: He got a safe! What he got a safe for if he keep the money under the counter? I tell him to open the safe and you run out the door!

MISTER: That take too long. I told you we just get in and get out. You see where he didn't want to open it.

KING: I was gonna make the motherfucker open it! Talking about he don't know the combination. He know the combination!

MISTER: The way it supposed to work is he see the gun and give you the money. It ain't supposed to go past that. If he willing to die over his money he deserve to have it.

KING: If he want to die over his money then let the motherfucker die. You can always get you some more money but you can't get another life. If he want to be that dumb . . . fuck him!

MISTER: What was you doing behind the counter?

KING: I got Tonya a ring! What's wrong with that?

MISTER: That's how you get caught, selling the jewelry.

KING: I ain't gonna sell it. I'm gonna give it to Tonya.

MISTER: How much we get?

(King pulls the pillowcase out from under his coat and begins to count the money.)

KING: You think anybody seen us?

MISTER: Just that man that came out that house. Look like he was going to his car. But he don't know why we was running.

KING: It ain't gonna take him long to find out. Did he get a good look at you?

MISTER: I looked at him real good but he just glanced at me. If he had looked at me real good I would have known it. How much we get?

KING: Three thousand, one hundred and sixty dollars.

MISTER: Seem like it ought to have been more.

KING: He probably had the rest of the money in the safe. I should have made him open it! I was making him open it and you run out the door!

MISTER: I just wanted to get out of there. I told you that take too long.

KING: That's where the money's at! Talking about he keep it under the counter. It's in the safe. The money's in the safe!

MISTER: I just wanted to get out of there.

KING: This ain't enough to do nothing with.

MISTER: It's more than we had. We each got fifteen hundred dollars.

KING: I'm trying to get fifteen thousand!

(*Stool Pigeon enters from the street. He has a paper bag. Above his left eye is a bandage.*)

How you doing, Stool Pigeon? How's them dogs? Getting enough to eat?

MISTER: Yeah, how you doing, Stool Pigeon?

STOOL PIGEON: They got sixty-three dollars. That's all I had. They took that. Then they burned up my newspapers. I wasn't gonna fight them on that sixty-three dollars but I tried to fight them on my newspapers.

KING: Who? What they look like?

STOOL PIGEON: Had on black hats.

MISTER: That sound like them dudes hang up around White-side Road. Wear them black hats and black sweatshirts.

KING: I'm gonna go up there and put my foot in their ass.

STOOL PIGEON: One of them kicked me in the head. Had to get six stitches. Right down there at Mercy Hospital. I had to wait while they sewed somebody else up. If it wasn't for the white man, what would I do? Nigger bust you up and the white man fix you up. If he wasn't there, what would I do? They kicked me in the side. It feel like it but the doctor say my ribs ain't broke. I'm gonna see if they put that in the paper. "Man Robbed of Sixty-Three Dollars. Busted Head but Ribs Okay." I'm gonna see if they put that in there.

KING: What you got in that bag?

STOOL PIGEON: This my papers. What's left of them. What them kids gonna do now? They burned up their history. They ain't gonna know what happened. They ain't gonna know how they got from tit to tat. You got to know that. They ain't gonna know nothing. I ask myself, "Why they do that?" I have to tell myself the truth. I don't know. If somebody know and they tell me then I'll know. But the truth is I don't know. I can't figure it out. (*He takes some ashes out of the bag and sprinkles them on the grave of the cat*) "For whosoever believeth, then shall I cause him to be raised into Eternal Life and magnify the Glory of My Father, the Lord God who made the firmament. Then shall Death flee and hide his face in darkness. For My Father ruleth over all things in his creation." If she coming back that'll help her. All you need now is some blood. Blood is life. You sprinkle some blood on there and if she ain't used up her nine lives Aunt Ester's coming back. (*He exits into the house*)

(*Mister takes a thousand dollars and gives it to King.*)

MISTER: Here. That's for the pot. I got five hundred dollars and I get paid this week. I don't want to die a poor man either.
KING: We almost got enough. I put in a thousand, that make eight. We can go see the man about renting the place.
MISTER: We got to do it soon. I can take off work again tomorrow.

(*Elmore enters.*)

ELMORE: Hey, fellows. I got a man want to buy a refrigerator.
KING: What model he want? You know some models cost two hundred and fifty dollars.
ELMORE: I don't know about no model and he ain't got but a hundred and seventy-five dollars.
KING: Naw, naw, it cost two hundred dollars.
MISTER: Do he got it now or do he have to go get it? 'Cause if he got to go get it he may as well get twenty-five dollars more.

ELMORE: He got it right now. Cash money. Say he wanna see the refrigerator.

KING: He can see it. He can see it when we dump it down on his doorstep. I told you we can't be letting nobody know where it is.

ELMORE: He want me to go look at it for him.

MISTER: We can't let nobody know. We ain't in this by ourselves. We got partners. We can't be letting nobody know our business.

KING: This kind of business is done on trust. Give me the hundred seventy-five dollars and I'll go get him a refrigerator. Brand-new. Still in the box.

ELMORE: He ain't gonna buy it without seeing it. He don't want to buy a pig in a poke.

KING: I don't know nothing about no pig. No poke either. It's two hundred dollars anyway. We giving him a break.

ELMORE: I get thirty dollars if I sell it. That's what we agreed on.

MISTER: Naw, we got to cut you back to twenty dollars. He ain't paying full price.

ELMORE: You ain't got to sell it to him at that price.

MISTER: I know. But if we do you can't expect to get your full commission.

ELMORE: All right, give me twenty. That's a hundred seventy-five for the refrigerator and twenty for me.

(Elmore hands King a hundred seventy-five dollars.)

KING: Here go your twenty. Where you want it delivered at? Who's the man?

ELMORE: Me. You can deliver it right here. That's for your mama.

MISTER: Naw, naw. We ain't gonna pay you to buy a refrigerator from us!

ELMORE: That's what you said. You said you'd give me twenty dollars if I sell one. I didn't say nothing about who I was gonna sell it to. That wasn't in the bargain.

MISTER: Well, then you got to pay two hundred dollars like everybody else.

ELMORE: I told you the man ain't had but a hundred seventy-five dollars. You said okay. What you care who the man is?

MISTER: Naw, that ain't right. What that look like? We paying you to buy a refrigerator from us.

ELMORE: That's what you agreed on. A man lives up to his word. Now, what you gonna be?

KING: That's all right, Mister. That was a good one, Elmore. I'm gonna remember that. I might get me a chance to use it.

MISTER: All right, Elmore. You got that. That's the last one.

ELMORE: I been doing this a long time, fellows. You got to look at all the angles and when you see a opening that will get you a little advantage . . . you got to take that. You wanna shoot some crap? Come on, let's shoot some crap.

MISTER: Naw, I ain't got my dice yet. I get me some dice, I'll shoot you.

ELMORE: I got some dice.

MISTER: Hey King, I got to go.

KING: Where you going? You ain't got nowhere to go.

MISTER: I'm going down the furniture store. Get me a TV. Get me a VCR. Get me a bed. I got these two women fighting over me. With one of them I can get it anytime I want. I'm working on the other one.

KING: I'll see you tomorrow.

(Mister exits.)

ELMORE: Life is funny. I keep trying to figure it out. One woman leave and two other trying to get in the door. Somebody going where somebody just left. That's what I think when I see people on the Greyhound. Somebody going where somebody just left. (He goes over and looks at the seeds) I bet nobody won't step on them seeds now. Not with that barbed wire there.

KING: Hey Elmore, do you see a halo around my head?

ELMORE: You mean like a light that's shining. I don't see nothing. That don't mean it ain't there. I'm the last one to ask about something like that.

  You turned out all right. Life throw a little bit of trouble at you just to keep you on your toes . . . but you turned out all right. I hear you had a little trouble. How much time you do down there?

KING: Seven years. I did seven years. I was supposed to do ten.

ELMORE: I did five. Five years in an Alabama penitentiary feels like fifteen.

KING: I see you ain't spent no time down at Western State Penitentiary.

ELMORE: I'm sixty-six years old. I ain't never had to use my pistol but once. It was enough for most people just knowing I had it. It was enough for me. I had to cut me a couple of people but I ain't never had to use my pistol but once. I was playing a heavy game back then too. I was leaning so far I had to try to hold on. My game was like a knife jabbing at you. Sometime I thought I might go over the edge and hurt myself. I never did fall until that thing with Leroy. Until then I was one of the most righteous motherfuckers you could find. I had my game together and was playing it. I don't know how I ended up in that barbershop with a gun in my hand.

KING: That the same thing with me and Pernell. I wasn't headed that way but that's where I ended up. If he hadn't called me "champ," my whole life would have been different.

ELMORE: They give me them five years and I was laying in that jail with my face turned to the wall. I ain't never slept like that. But that Leroy thing just grabbed hold of me. I took away too much. I took away all his women. He ain't gonna have no more of them. I took away all his pleasure. I took away all his pain. And you need that, otherwise you living half of life.

KING: Life without pain ain't worth living.

ELMORE: I took that away. Everything he was gonna learn. I took that. I like to learn things. Even the hard way. It makes the rest of life make more sense. You get to thinking pretty soon you might get a handle on it. Then something happen to prove you wrong. Now you got to start all over again. See if you can get it right. I took that away. I took away too much. When you add it all up I could have just went on and left. It didn't cost me nothing. That was a little thing.

KING: People try to say Pernell calling me "champ" was a little thing. But I don't see it that way.

ELMORE: It didn't seem like it at the time. But it was a little thing in the grand scheme of things. I laid with my face to the wall for two years before I could turn over. Ruby used to write me letters. Her and my mama. That's the only way I got to where I could turn my back to the wall. I was all right after that. I had made my peace with God but I found out later you got to make peace with yourself. See, when you pulled that trigger you done something. You done something more than most other people. You know more about life 'cause you done been to that part of it. Most people don't never get over on that side . . . that part of life. They live on the safe side. But see . . . you done been God. Death is something he do. God decide when somebody ready. Not you. He decide when he want somebody. God don't like that, you thinking you him. He cut you loose.

KING: Anybody kill somebody is living without God. You ain't even got no right to pray. When Mama Louise died I was standing around the bedside. She told me she was gonna leave me in the hands of God. She didn't know that I had already messed that up.

ELMORE: Anybody kill somebody is on their own.

KING: I don't know about you and Leroy but Pernell made me kill him. Pernell called me "champ." I told him my name's King. He say, "Yeah, champ." I go on. I don't say nothing. I told myself, "He don't know." He don't know my daddy killed a man for calling him out of his name. He don't know he fucking with King Hedley II. I got the atomic bomb as far as he's concerned. And I got to use it. They say God looks after fools and drunks. I used to think that was true. But seeing as how he was both . . . I don't know anymore. He called me "champ" and I didn't say nothing. I put him on probation. Told myself he don't know but I'm gonna give him a chance to find out. If he find out and come and tell me he's sorry then I'll let him live. I'm gonna fuck him up. I'm gonna bust both his kneecaps. But I'm gonna let him live. Saturday. I don't know why it's always on a Saturday. Saturday I went up to buy me some potatoes. I say, "I want to have some mashed potatoes." I told Neesi, say, "You get the milk and butter and I'll get the potatoes." I went right up there to Hester's on Wylie. I went up there and got me ten pound of potatoes. I started to get twenty but they only had one bag and it was tore, the bag was tore. I didn't want them to spill out on the way home. If I had been carrying twenty pounds of potatoes maybe I would have went home a shorter way. I say, "Let me breeze by Center Avenue on my way home and let me see if I see Charlie. He owe me twenty dollars and if he pay me that might bring me some luck." I got halfway down there and I seen Pernell. First thing I tell myself is, "I ain't gonna be nobody's champ today." I fix that hard in my head and I try to walk past him. I didn't want to ignore him so I say, "How you doing, Pernell?" I don't really care how he doing. I'm just being polite like Mama Louise taught me. No sooner than the words got out my mouth then I felt something hot on my face. A hot flash and then something warm and wet. This nigger done cut me! He hit me with that razor and I froze. I didn't know what happened. It was like somebody turned on a light and it seem like everything stood still and I could see him smiling. Then he ran. I didn't know which way he ran. I was still blinded by that light. It took the doctor four hours and a hundred and twelve stitches to sew me up. I say, "That's all right, the King is still here." But I figure that scar got to mean something. I can't take it off. It's part of me now. I figure it's got to mean something. As long as Pernell was still walking around it wasn't nothing but a scar. I had to give it some meaning.

It wasn't but two weeks later and I'm thinking about this thing. I'm thinking what it gonna mean to everybody. I thought about his mama. I thought the whole thing out. It ain't easy to take somebody's life. I told myself, "It's me or him," even though I knew that was a lie. I saw his funeral. I heard the preacher. I saw the undertaker. I saw the grave-diggers. I saw the flowers. And then I see his woman. That's the hardest part. She know him better than anybody. She know what makes him bleed. She know why he breathes, what he sound like when he wakes up in the morning. She know when he's hungry and what will satisfy him. She know everything what nobody else don't know. It was hard but I told myself she got to suffer. She got to play the widow. She got to cry the tears.

About two weeks later I saw Pernell going into Irv's bar. He went straight back to the phone booth. I don't know who he was calling but that was the last call he made. I saw my scar in the window of the phone booth. I tapped on the glass. He turned and looked and froze right there. The first bullet hit him in the mouth. I don't know where the other fourteen went. The only regret is I didn't get away. I didn't get away with murder that time. You always regret the one you don't get away with. Cost me seven years of my life. But I done got smarter. The next one's gonna be self-defense. The next one ain't gonna cost me nothing.

ELMORE: Pernell didn't know when he called you "champ" he had set himself on the road to a bad end. That's the road you want to avoid. You don't want to look up and find yourself traveling on that road. Now you talk about you and Pernell . . . let me tell you about me and Leroy. You need to know this. Now there was this big crap game. The Mullins brothers . . .

(Ruby enters from the house.)

Hey, I was looking to take you out. Let's go out. What was the name of that club out in East Liberty?

RUBY: That's been gone.

ELMORE: That was a nice little club. We had us a good time there. Come on, let's go out somewhere.

RUBY: I ain't got nothing to wear.

ELMORE: You with me. The only time you got to worry about what to wear is if you out there looking. You ain't looking for nobody. Come on, put on anything.

RUBY: Come on, let's go to the bar around the corner.

ELMORE: I can't go right now. I got to go back down there and see if these niggers got any more money. I'll come back and then we can go out.

RUBY: Where you going?

ELMORE: I'm going in here to change clothes. I can't go back down there wearing the same clothes.

(Tonya enters from the house. She is dressed for work.)

Hey, Tonya. You on your way to work?

TONYA: Yeah, I'm going down here to pull these cards for the insurance people. That's the only way I pay my bills.

(Elmore exits into the house.)

RUBY: You all go on and make up. You need each other.

KING: I ain't got nothing to make up about.

RUBY: Go on now. *(She exits into the house)*

KING: Tonya. Here.

(King gives Tonya some money.)

TONYA: What's this? Where'd you get this from? *(She counts the money)* This is five hundred dollars. Where'd you get it from?

KING: I got it from the same place Mellon get his. You don't ask him where he get his from.

TONYA: Here. I don't want it.

KING: What you talking about you don't want it?

TONYA: You done stole it somewhere. You going back to jail. You gonna be right down there with J.C. Talking about you wanna have a baby and time he one or two years old you look up and he ain't gonna see you again till he's twelve. I got to sleep by myself. Naw, you take it and keep it. I don't want it. I don't want you to be saying you did it for me. Don't do it for me. I ain't gonna make the same mistake twice. I'm working every day, I'll pay my bills the best way I can. But I ain't gonna have you sitting down there in the jail talking about you did it for me.

KING: Money green. That's all you got to know. What difference it make? Money is money. They make it with a machine. I ain't got no machine. I got to get mine the best way I can. It's legal. That's what it say on there. Say it's legal for all debts public and private. That's all anybody care about money. Can you spend it.

TONYA: I got to go to work. But I'm telling you . . . don't do it for me. You hear me, King. Don't do it for me. (*She exits the yard*)

KING (*Calling after her*): Who else I'm gonna do it for? Money's money, woman! Who else I'm gonna do it for?

(*The lights go down on the scene.*)

SCENE 3

The lights come up on Ruby and Tonya in the yard.

RUBY: Where's King?

TONYA: He said he was going out to Homewood to look for Pernell's cousin. He walking around carryin' that gun. Now you got to wonder if he ever gonna come through the door again or not. Every time he go out somewhere I hold my breath. I'm tired of it. I'm suffocating myself. I done told him if he go back to jail I'm through with it. I gonna pack up my little stuff and leave. I ain't goin' through that again. I ain't visiting any more jailhouses.

RUBY: That was the same with Elmore down in East St. Louis. They don't know it's hard on you. They don't think about that. I buried one man, I don't want to bury no more. King just like Hedley. Hedley had his own way about him. He wanted to be somebody and couldn't figure out how.

TONYA: I wish I had known Hedley. 'Cause I can see that's half of King's problem. He try and do everything the way he think Hedley would do it. Louise used to tell him all the time, "Be yourself. That's enough."

RUBY: She used to tell me the same thing. That's what I tried to do. Even when I didn't know who I was, I guessed at it. Sometimes I was right and sometimes I got it all wrong. I used to be really something back then. All the men was after me. They use to crawl all over me. That's when I was singing. I used to sing with Walter Kelly's band. I always did like to sing. Seem like that was a better way of talking. You could put more meaning to it.

TONYA: I let Aretha do my singing for me. I can't do it better than her so I need to shut up.

RUBY: Walter Kelly was a big man with jet black hair. Brown-skinned man played a trumpet and I sang in his band for a while. He tried to make love to me but I didn't want no part of him 'cause he was too good-looking and he already had a gang of women. Everybody expected 'cause I sang in his band that he could have do with me like he wanted. He thought that at one time himself but I got him straight on that. We was sitting in his car. He had a car with a top you could put down. We was having a drink and just laughing and singing and fooling around when he put his hand under my dress. I had men put their hand under my dress before. They want to see what you got. They like to see how it fit in their hand. They say they can tell what kind of woman you is. Walter Kelly got his hand all the way up under my dress and he touched me there. I told him to stop. He just laughed. We was drinking from a pint bottle. I took the bottle and broke it on the car handle. I cut my hand pretty bad but I put the glass up to his throat. Blood was running all down my hand and everywhere. I told him to lick it. I told him I wanted him to taste my blood 'cause if he didn't move his hand from under my dress I was gonna taste his. I rubbed my hand all over his face. There was blood everywhere. My hand looked like it wasn't gonna stop bleeding. He moved his hand and I got out of the car. I found out later I was on my period and I got mad. I told myself I wished I had cut him 'cause there wasn't nobody's blood in the car but mine.

TONYA: You should have cut him.

RUBY: He never did mess with me no more. We became good friends. Walter Kelly . . . I left out of East St. Louis and lost touch with him. I hear tell he died about eight years ago. I felt real sad when I heard it. I stopped singing about two years after that night in the car. I just stopped for no reason. I did it to myself. Said I don't want to sing no more. It had done lost something. The melody or something I couldn't tell. I just know it stopped having any meaning for me. There was lots of things like that. Where the meaning all got mixed up with something else.

After I quit singing my hair turned gray. My hair turned gray and I didn't even know it. I was staying in a room up on Wooster Street. I went upstairs to the bathroom and seen I had gray hair. Seem like I didn't have nothing to show for it. I said, "I'm gonna die and ain't nobody gonna miss me." I got dressed and said, "I'm going go find me a man . . . if nothing else he might miss me in the morning when I'm gone." We went to the Ellis Hotel. He had a mustache and a big hat. It was that hat that made him look nice. He was a rough man. He turned me over his knee and spanked me. That was the first time anybody ever did that. He asked me did I like it. I told him I didn't know, he'd have to do it again. It had been a long time since anybody had touched me. It kinda felt good. Just to know I had been touched. We had a good time. Then it was time to go. I asked him if he was gonna miss me. He said he was, but I don't know if he was telling the truth. I went back and looked in the mirror and my hair was still gray. I told myself, "I'm still a woman. Gray hair and all."

(Stool Pigeon enters carrying flowers and peanuts.)

STOOL PIGEON: They had to take Aunt Ester back down there. They wanna do an autopsy but Mr. Eli fighting them on that. The coroner say he want to see if he can figure out what made her live so long. He don't know she died too soon. She wasn't supposed to die at all. She wasn't but three hundred and sixty-six years old. *(He goes over to the cat's grave)*

TONYA: You done buried that cat out there . . . why don't you just leave it alone?

STOOL PIGEON: I give her some peanuts. Some goobers. That's what my mama called them. See if God satisfied with that. *(He lays the flowers on the grave)*

>The Mighty God
>His name shall be called Wonderful
>Who made the fire
>May all that is passed be joined together
>The Mighty God
>Made the wind
>Mighty is His name
>Who made the water
>Called man out of the dust
>The Mighty God
>Made the firmament
>Called forth Lazarus
>The Mighty God
>Who makes hallowed the ground
>The Mighty God
>You a bad motherfucker.

(Turning back to Tonya and Ruby) They got goats out at the zoo but they won't give me none. I went out there and asked them. They told us they want to keep them for the kids. I'm on my way to ask Hop. See if he loan me his truck to go out to one of them farms and get a fatted calf. Time's running out. But I'm gonna get some blood on that grave. *(He exits the yard)*

RUBY: That old fool. You watch and see if he don't end up in Mayview.

(Mister enters.)

MISTER: King here?

TONYA: I thought King was with you.

MISTER: He said he was going down to the courthouse. Hop was having his hearing today to see if they was gonna give him the contract.

TONYA: I hope he don't go down there acting a fool. I know King. He liable to go down there and cuss out the judge. I done told him. I'll pack up my little stuff in a minute. *(She exits into the house)*

RUBY: What you got there in your hand? Look like a tin cup.

MISTER: You wasn't supposed to see it. This a derringer Elmore sold me. Only it's too big to hide in your hand. Everybody can see it.

RUBY: That's what I need. In case somebody mess with me. These kids is something else. They robbed Stool Pigeon and robbed and beat up that little old woman live on Casset Street. Put her in the hospital. I need something like that in case somebody mess with me. I'm gonna get me one.

MISTER: Here . . . you can have this one. Only thing, you have to pull back the hammer if you want to fire it. *(He gives her the derringer)* Here go two bullets. That's all I got. If you need some more I'll get them for you.

RUBY: I wanna see somebody mess with me now.

MISTER: They got Little Buddy Will's mother in jail. She shot the boy who she say killed her son. She shot him but only thing she didn't kill him. He in the hospital. They say he might make it.

RUBY: It serves him right. I don't blame her. She shouldn't have to do a day in jail. They ought to give her a medal.

(King enters.)

MISTER: Hey, King.

KING: Where Tonya?

RUBY: What they say down there about Hop's contract?

KING: They gave him the contract. They thought he was gonna walk away like most niggers. When he went to court they couldn't do nothin' but give him the contract.

RUBY *(Calling)*: Tonya!

(Tonya enters from the house.)

TONYA: Where you been?

KING: I went down to the courthouse. They give Hop the contract. *(He goes over to his seeds)*

MISTER: They getting bigger.

KING: If Elmore hadn't stepped on them they would be bigger than that. I told Ruby dirt was dirt. Like my dirt ain't good enough.

RUBY: I didn't think they was gonna grow. Your daddy knew about growing things. I guess if anybody could get them to grow it would be you. You need some water. Here . . . I'll get you some water. *(She exits into the house)*

MISTER: They supposed to deliver my furniture today. I'll see you all later.

(Mister exits the yard. Tonya starts into the house.)

KING: Tonya. Look here a minute. I went out to visit Neesi's grave for the last time. I can't carry her no more. I told her I am through visiting but I ain't through remembering.

I talked to her for a long while. The gate was locked when I was leaving. They lock it up at seven o'clock so I had to go out the back. I never went out the back before. I was walking through there and I seen Pernell's grave. It took me by surprise. He got a marker. It say, "Pernell Sims, 1949–1974. Father. Son. Brother." I didn't even know Pernell had no kids.

TONYA: He had that baby by that girl that live up on Whiteside Road. A little boy.

KING: His daddy laying out in the cemetery. That's like me and my daddy. I wasn't but three years old when he died. I told myself Pernell fucked up. If he hadn't called me "champ," he'd still be alive. But then I had something to do with that too. I didn't expect to see his grave. I never thought about where Pernell was buried. I looked at it a long time. I tried to walk away but I couldn't. I found myself wondering what color his casket was. They say your hair keep growing. I wonder if that's true.

TONYA: Your hair and your fingernails too.

KING: I tried to see Pernell laying up there with his old simple self. You ever see Pernell's son?

TONYA: He go to McKelvy school.

KING: Tonya. Look at that. That dirt's hard. That dirt's rocky. But it still growing. It's gonna open up and its gonna be beautiful. I ain't never looked at no flower before. I ain't never tried to grow none. I was coming out the drugstore and they had them seeds on the counter. I say, "I'm gonna try this. Grow Tonya some flowers. I ain't got nothing to lose but a dollar. I'll pay a dollar to see how it turn out." Ruby told me they wasn't gonna grow. Made me feel like I should have left them there at the drugstore. But then they grew. Elmore stepped on them and they still growing. That's what made me think of Pernell. Pernell stepped on me and I pulled his life out by the root. What does that make me? It don't make me a big man. Most people see me coming and they go the other way. They wave from across the street.

People look at their hands funny after they shake my hand. They try to pretend they don't see my scar when that's all they looking at. I used to think Pernell did that to me. But I did it to myself. Pernell put that scar on my face, but I put the bigger mark on myself. That's why I need this baby, not 'cause I took something out the world but because I wanna put something in it. Let everybody know I was here. You got King Hedley II and then you got King Hedley III. Got rocky dirt. Got glass and bottles. But it still deserve to live. Even if you do have to call the undertaker. Even if somebody come along and pull it out by the root. It still deserve to live. It still deserve that chance. I'm here and I ain't going nowhere. I need to have that baby. Do you understand?

TONYA: You walking around with a gun, looking to kill somebody, talking about you wanna have a baby. You either gonna end up dead or in jail. That's what's wrong with Natasha now. Her daddy been in jail for half her life. She wouldn't know him if she saw him. She don't even know what a daddy is. I don't want that for my children. What kind of mother that make me. People talk about me now. "Tonya like them roguish thugs." I married you because I loved you and I thought you understood something about life. I thought I could make a life with you. I didn't know you was gonna start yourself on a path that was gonna lead you right back down to the penitentiary.

KING: I ain't gonna stop living. The world ain't gonna change and all of a sudden get better because I be somebody's daddy. Pernell's cousin ain't gonna go away just 'cause I'm gonna be somebody's daddy. I can't go and get no job just because I'm somebody's daddy. Quite naturally I got more to think about now. But I ain't gonna stop living. I'm just trying to do my job. Get you the things you want.

TONYA: King, you don't understand. I don't want everything. That's not why I'm living . . . to want things. I done lived thirty-five years without things. I got enough for me. I just want to wake up in the bed beside you in the morning.

I don't need things. I saw what they cost. I can live without them and be happy. I ain't asking you to stop living. The things I want you can't buy with money. And it seem like they be the hardest to get. Why? When they be the simplest. Do your job but understand what it is. It ain't for you to go out of here and steal money to get me things. Your job is to be around so this baby can know you its daddy. Do that. For once, somebody do that. Be that. That's how you be a man, anything else I don't want.

(King doesn't respond. The lights go down on the scene.)

Scene 4

The lights come up on King and Mister in the yard. King is polishing the machete.

MISTER: When you start back to work?

KING: Six o'clock tomorrow morning. If they don't bury Aunt Ester tomorrow. I asked Mr. Eli. He say he'd let me know. He don't know when they gonna get a chance to bury her. They won't give back the body. The coroner tryin' to figure out what made her live so long.

MISTER: Hester's is still closed. You got to go all the way up on Herron Avenue if you want to get some milk and bread.

KING: Half the places around here is closed. They ain't gonna open until after her funeral. What they say when you quit?

MISTER: They said, "Bye." Told me I could pick up my paycheck on Tuesday.

KING: If I was you I would have been done quit.

MISTER: I was waitin' till they got the order. They got the order and still wouldn't give me my raise.

KING: That's all right. We get the video store and you won't need no job.

(Elmore and Ruby enter. Ruby is wearing the necklace Elmore gave her, and she is dressed in her best dress.)

ELMORE: Hey, fellows.

RUBY: Me and Elmore gonna get married! We went down and got the license.

MISTER: Hey Elmore, do you need a best man? I'll be the best man at Miss Ruby's wedding.

RUBY: We going to the Justice of the Peace. We ain't gonna have no church wedding. I'm too old for a church wedding.

MISTER: I don't care if it's the justice of the peace. They don't all the time have a best man but sometime they do.

RUBY: Where's Tonya.

KING: She in the house.

(Ruby exits into the house.)

Hey Elmore, look here. Today's your lucky day.

(King sticks the machete in the ground with the seeds. He takes a diamond ring from his pocket and hands it to Elmore.)

I don't want but a hundred dollars. I was gonna give that to Tonya but I changed my mind. That's a whole karat. You can look at it and see it's worth eight or nine hundred dollars.

ELMORE: I'll give you seventy-five.

KING: Naw, I got to get a hundred.

(Elmore gives King a hundred dollars. King offers Mister fifty dollars.)

MISTER: Naw, you keep it.

(Ruby enters from the house.)

RUBY: Where's Tonya?

KING: She must have went up to her mother's.

ELMORE: Hey, Ruby . . . come here. Give me your hand.

(Elmore puts the ring on Ruby's finger.)

RUBY: Where you get this from? Look at this! I can't see! I got a diamond ring! I can't see nothing! That light blind me. You supposed to say you love me or something.

ELMORE: That ring say that and a whole lot more.

MISTER: You supposed to say, "I do."

ELMORE: I love you. I do.

MISTER: You may now kiss the bride.

(Tonya enters from the street.)

RUBY: Tonya! Me and Elmore's getting married! I got me a diamond ring! *(She shows Tonya the ring)*

TONYA: Oh, Miss Ruby! I'm glad for you. You finally gonna do it!

(Tonya embraces Ruby.)

RUBY: We got the license. We just went down and got it. Elmore got to go to Cleveland to pick up some money, then we gonna get married.

ELMORE: It ain't gonna take me but three days. I'm going right down there and come back.

RUBY: Come on, let's waltz.

ELMORE: We ain't got no music.

RUBY: You don't need no music. Can't you hear the music. I can hear the music.

(Ruby and Elmore dance a waltz. The music plays softly in Ruby's head.)

"The Mattie Dee Waltz." That was the prettiest song. I never will forget that.

(Stool Pigeon enters from the street. He stops.)

STOOL PIGEON: Now that's something I ain't never done. Dance without no music.

RUBY: Canewell. Me and Elmore gonna get married. (*She shows Stool Pigeon her ring*)

STOOL PIGEON: I always did believe in love. A woman went a thousand miles to see a man! That's in the Bible. The Queen of Sheba went a thousand miles to see King Solomon. He told her say, she was dark and comely, said her eyes were like the Morning Star and her hair the Crowning Raiments of the Night. Say her lips were like rubies, and her skin as smooth as a baby's ass! A woman went a thousand miles to see a man! Who would have thought!

(*Stool Pigeon exits. Ruby grabs King.*)

RUBY: Come on, let me teach you how to waltz.

KING: I don't want to learn how to waltz. What am I gonna do with that.

MISTER: That means you sophisticated. If you know how to waltz that means you sophisticated. My mama was sophisticated.

RUBY: Come on, let me teach you . . .

(*Ruby and King begin to waltz.*)

Ain't nothing to it. Put you foot back like this and just mark out a square. Come on, put you foot back like this. It's easy to waltz. Leroy Slater taught me how to waltz. We used to waltz all across the county.

KING: I don't want to waltz across the county. I don't want to be but so sophisticated.

RUBY: Come on, just mark out a little square.

(*King stops.*)

KING: I need some music. I can't dance without no music.

RUBY: You don't need no music. Ask Elmore. You got to hear it in your head.

(She starts waltzing by herself, the music playing in her head, and for one brief moment, all the possibilities of life are shining. Stool Pigeon enters from his house and sits on the steps eating a bowl of chili. Ruby sings:)

> Dear Mattie Dee
> I'm writing to say
> My love for you
> Grows and grows each day.

"The Mattie Dee Waltz." Me and Leroy used to waltz all over the county. That was the prettiest song.

ELMORE: Leroy was trying to play a riff on my tune. He didn't know I wrote the motherfucker!

(Ruby stops dancing.)

RUBY: Come on, now. We was having fun.

ELMORE: Called hisself a hustler but he didn't know what a hustler was. I'm a hustler. When I met him he had on a dirty shirt and didn't know it.

RUBY: You always got to put him down.

ELMORE: I'm telling the truth about the man. Did he have on a dirty shirt?

RUBY: I don't know if he did or not.

ELMORE: I'm telling you he did. I know. When I met Leroy Slater he had on a dirty shirt. His heels were run over and he ain't had but five dollars in his pocket.

RUBY: Elmore! Stop it!

ELMORE: I'm talking to the man. How you gonna tell me who to talk to? Leroy had a disposition that was hard to take. Everybody tell you that. He got on everybody's nerves. When I met him he was living up on Peach Way in Montgomery,

Alabama. He didn't have no woman. He had on a dirty shirt and didn't know it. Now me and Ruby had been staying together but it seem like we just couldn't get along. She don't understand I'm glad to see her. She bring me love. Why wouldn't I be glad to see her? But if she bring me grief . . .

KING: You got to move on.

ELMORE: Grief don't bring you nothing but tears. A man's gonna cry over a woman. That's all there is to it. That's why she's called a woman. She bring woe. But if she bring too much woe, you gotta move on. We said it the best thing for us to split up. We said good-bye with tears in our eyes. I told her, "May God bless you everywhere you go." I ain't gonna stand in her way of love 'cause I don't want nobody to stand in mine.

RUBY: You didn't know what you had.

ELMORE: I told you I wasn't ready for you!

RUBY: Leroy knew. That's why you killed him.

ELMORE: The nigger had my fifty dollars!

RUBY: That's what you say. You say that 'cause you don't want to admit the truth. He ain't told me nothing about owing you no fifty dollars.

ELMORE: I don't care if he told you or not. The nigger owed me fifty dollars.

RUBY: Elmore think it's all about him. Leroy wasn't like that.

ELMORE: It is about me! Who else it gonna be about? I got to live my life. I can't live it for nobody else. It is about me! How it gonna be otherwise? I look out from standing over here. You over there. We see different things. If we can't agree on what we see I got to find somebody who do. Leroy was looking to find anybody he can get. He hooked up with Ruby and that disposition got worse. He frown up every time he see me.

KING: That's on him.

ELMORE: I ain't got no hard feeling about nothing. Ruby was grown and I didn't have no woman 'cause I didn't want one. All right now, there was a big crap game. The Mullin brothers . . . there was three of them but only two had showed up. They come on through with about ten thousand dollars. They figure they'd use that to clean everybody out and then move on to the next city. If you wasn't careful every nigger in Montgomery would be broke and it be hard times for the next three months.

The crap game had been going on for about four days and the Mullin brothers was losing. After three days they called Mobile and sent for the other brother. I had a little bit of money and a fellow named Ward Henry come and got me . . . asked me to come and go down to the crap game with him. He said, "Let's stop and get Leroy Slater." He say Leroy knew how to handle a gun and in case the Mullin brothers wanted to get nasty we could back one another up. I say all right, and we went on up there where he was staying with Ruby. Leroy say he ain't had no money. I told him I'd loan him fifty dollars but he'd have to split half his winnings with me. That's usually the way that work.

MISTER: That's how it work all the time. Half your winnings.

ELMORE: If you win you don't mind 'cause without that loan you wouldn't have nothing. This way you got something.

MISTER: Even if it ain't nothing but a little bit.

ELMORE: Leroy say okay and we go on down there. The Mullin brothers had a run of bad luck. It ain't had nothing to do with their skill as a gambler. It was just bad luck. We left out of there all three winners. Leroy had two hundred and fifty dollars. He took and give me a hundred. I didn't say nothing, I just kept my hand out. I asked him for my fifty dollars. He said it was in the hundred. I told him no. Win, lose or draw, he still owed me fifty dollars. I told him say if he didn't pay me the fifty dollars I was gonna tell everybody I know. We argued about it and he turned and walked off calling me a bunch of names.

MISTER: The fifty dollars supposed to be in the hundred.

KING: Naw. The fifty dollars is a loan.

ELMORE: Right. You still got to pay the loan.

MISTER: You paying it! It's in the hundred! It's got to be.

KING: Naw. Naw. He owe him fifty dollars.

MISTER: How you gonna owe another fifty dollars? When you done give the man a hundred? It ain't like you ain't give him nothing back. He got fifty dollars more than he had before.

KING: He supposed to have a hundred more. Half you winning is what the loan cost but you still got to pay back the loan.

ELMORE: That's the stake.

MISTER: Stake or no stake, you loan me fifty dollars. I give you half my winning. We straight. I don't owe you nothing else.

KING: I'd put my foot up his ass if he didn't give me my fifty dollars.

RUBY: He didn't tell me he owed Elmore no fifty dollars. He told me he had won some money and he was gonna buy a new radio.

ELMORE: He was gonna buy it with my fifty dollars. I would have bought a new radio too.

RUBY: I don't know what he was buying it with. He say he won some money in a crap game with the Mullin brothers. He was glad 'cause he left the game just in time. Say the Mullin brothers got mad and started shooting up the place.

ELMORE: That was two days later. After the third brother came in from Mobile. They said they had been cheated and wanted their money back. That ain't had nothing to do with my fifty dollars.

RUBY: I'm just telling you what he told me.

ELMORE: But you don't know. You need to shut up if you talking what you don't know. That ain't had nothing to do with my fifty dollars. I went around telling everybody Leroy owed me fifty dollars. I figured I'd shame him into paying me. I told everybody I saw. All right. I was in this bar . . . Big Jake's Rendezvous Lounge. Leroy come and saw me. I thought he was gonna pay me my fifty dollars. I spoke to him and the next thing I knew he had pulled a gun on me, telling me he was gonna kill me if I kept putting the bad mouth on him. Now I didn't see the pistol when he pulled it on me. It caught me by surprise. I wasn't looking for that.

He shoved it in my face. Held it right between my eyes. I'm supposed to be a dead man 'cause he was supposed to pull the trigger. That's the first thing you learn about carrying a pistol. When you pull it, you better use it.

KING: He owe you fifty dollars and now he wanna chump you off in a crowded bar. If you do something like that you supposed to do it in a dark alley. You ain't supposed to do it in a crowded bar.

ELMORE: Now everybody looking at me trying to figure out what I'm gonna do. I went home and laid across the bed. I couldn't see where my life was going. I said I was gonna make a change. My life seem like it was empty. I got up and went and looked in the closet. I had seventeen suits and fourteen pair of shoes. Had eight or nine hats. I went and looked in the kitchen. I had a box of grits, a box of Morton's salt and two cans of pork and beans. I looked in my pocket. I had three hundred and forty-six dollars. I told myself that will get me anywhere Greyhound go. I took and pawned my hats. It was like putting them in storage. I was gonna come back for them. I went down to Greyhound and looked up on the board. I wanted to go to Cleveland but they had too many rough-house niggers down there. I didn't want all that, so I bought me a ticket to Cincinnati. That was on Tuesday. My rent was paid up till Friday and I figured I'd stay till then. I went around there and I ran into Ruby. I almost didn't recognize her. She walking around with a new dress. New hairdo. New shoes. I asked her where Leroy was. She said he was at the barbershop.

RUBY: You asked me to go to Cincinnati with you. I told you I wanted to see if me and Leroy could make it and you got mad.

ELMORE: I told you all right, if that's what you wanted. We had a drink. We laughed and talked. I told you I was going to Cincinnati and I hoped to see you again in the world somewhere. Wasn't nothing to get mad about. You was grown.

RUBY: Said you couldn't live without me. That you'd rather be dead. You asked me to go to Cincinnati with you. I told you no and you got mad and jealous of Leroy and went up there and killed him.

ELMORE: I went up there to tell him I was leaving and to forget about the fifty dollars. I figured I'd clean that up before I left. So there wouldn't be no hard feelings.

KING: I would have went up there, got my fifty dollars. He got your money . . . your woman . . . and he done chumped you off. He living dangerous.

ELMORE: Now, life is funny. You can only know so much about it. What you know at any given moment is what you need to know. If everything go like it's supposed to go, you gonna find out something else. If you willing and you need to know. When Leroy pulled that gun on me it gave me a headache. It wouldn't go away. Sometime it was all you could do to stand up. Gator was cutting his hair and Leroy was sitting in the chair laughing. I told myself something wrong. I'm walking around with a headache and he sitting up in the chair laughing. I started to walk away and Gator seen me and waved at me. That's when I walked in. I walked into the barbershop. Gator looked at me. He said, "Hey Elmore, what you got going?" Leroy was surprised to see me. My hand come out of my pocket. Gator told me later he thought I was gonna pay him some money I owed him. My hand come out with the gun. Gator took a step back. Leroy started to get out the chair. He was coming straight at me when I fired the gun. Gator said, "Damn, Elmore. Damn." The bullet hit him right smack in the middle of the forehead. That was the first bullet. I couldn't stop firing. Blood went everywhere. A piece of his skull bounced off the mirror and landed about ten feet away. I found myself wondering what that was. I didn't find out till later.

KING: Serve the motherfucker right!

RUBY: King.

ELMORE: I didn't say anything, I just walked out. Got outside and said, "Now what? That's over. Now what?" The bottom had fallen out of everything. Everything I had ever done in my life seemed small. I stood there looking up and down the street trying to figure out which way to go. I started shaking. My whole body started shaking. I tried to stop it from shaking but I couldn't. I started crying. My whole body shaking and tears just running down my face. Somebody come up and asked me what had happened and if I was all right. I started walking home. I don't know what happened to the gun. They never did find it. I believe I must have dropped it when I was shaking. I got home and sat down. All of a sudden I got sleepy. I couldn't keep my eyes open. I fell asleep in the chair and the next thing I knew it was morning of a brand-new day. I got up and started to cook my breakfast and it come up on me that something was wrong. The sun was coming through the kitchen window and it bounced off the handle of the frying pan, and that's what made me think something was wrong. I had seen that flash in the barbershop. When Leroy stood up he pulled out a gun as he was coming toward me. I stepped back and seen that flash and pulled the trigger. That's the first I remembered what had happened. I started crying again. I didn't know if it was a dream or not. I went and tried to find Gator but the barbershop was closed. I went up and saw Ruby. She say Leroy hadn't come home. She asked me what the matter was, and I told her I didn't know. I was on my way back up to see Gator when the police arrested me. I told them I didn't do nothing, I had just got out of bed. They told me they had witnesses say I killed Leroy Slater last night in the barbershop. I asked them where the body was. Show me the body. Told them I wanted proof I had killed somebody.

RUBY: They showed me the body. They come up and got me. His sister had gone to Mobile and they asked me to come down and see if it was him. I didn't want to look. I grabbed hold my arm and just squeezed. He had his mouth open. That's what I always will remember. Wasn't much more there. He was shot five times in the head. I looked away and something told me to look back. One shot had hit him in the nose and it just wasn't there no more. I don't know where it was. It wasn't on his face. They asked me did I know him. I told them, naw, I didn't know him, I ain't had a chance to find out too much about him. I told them I knew who it was. "That's Leroy Slater. I was living with him at 131 Warren Street." They asked me to sign some papers. One man told me he was sorry. I left out of there and walked on back home. That was the saddest day.

I couldn't look at Elmore after I found out what he had done. Even though I loved him, it was a long time before I could look at him. I felt so sad. I said I was gonna quit living. I stole away and cried. I didn't want nobody to see me. I felt like I was about to lose my mind. I cried and then I dried my eyes. Then I'd cry again. Seem like the world had gone crazy. Then everything stopped. They carried him on out there and put him in the ground. Leroy Slater. A good man. I never will forget him. They say life have its own rhythm. I wish it didn't have none like that. That was the saddest I ever been.

ELMORE: Leroy tried to play a game he didn't know how to play. He didn't know the rules. He tried to lead with the ace and didn't know I had the trump. If he knew that, he would have played his hand a different way. Now, that's how Leroy Slater got killed. That's how that went. I told you that part. Now your mother can tell you the rest.

RUBY: Elmore!

ELMORE: Tell him!

RUBY: Why you wanna do that? Why you wanna bring that up?

(*Ruby begins hitting Elmore.*)

Why you wanna do that?

ELMORE: Tell him!

RUBY: He don't need to know that! Why you wanna do this to me?

ELMORE: Tell him! He need to know.
KING: What? Tell me what?
RUBY: No! No!
ELMORE: That was your daddy. Leroy was you daddy.

(*Ruby continues to hit Elmore, but with little strength or purpose.*)

RUBY: Why you wanna do that?
KING: Tell me. Tell me.
RUBY: I was gonna carry that to my grave. You didn't need to know that.

(*King picks up the machete, turns and walks out of the yard.*)

TONYA: King.

(*The lights go down to black.*)

SCENE 5

The lights come up on Mister, Ruby and Tonya in the yard.

TONYA: Did you look down on Centre?
MISTER: I looked in all the places we be. I don't know but I think if you go out to the cemetery you'll find him. He go out to visit Neesi's grave. He always do that when something happen. Then when he come back he be a new man. Somebody kill your daddy, that seem like blood for blood to me. I know King. That's just what he thinking. He just want to think about it a while. Elmore need to go on to Cleveland if he wanna get there. Otherwise somebody gonna have to bury him. I know King. Your blood is your blood and ain't nothing thicker than that. King be looking for ways to prove it. Seem like this happened 'cause he looking for it to hap-

pen. Some things are like that. If you try and take King's honor he'll kill you. Whether he right or wrong.

RUBY: King don't need to be killing nobody.

MISTER: Ain't nothing else he can do. King got his job to do. What's his daddy gonna say?

RUBY: His daddy dead. What's he gonna say? He can't say nothing.

MISTER: King got to say it for him. He got to look in the mirror and see what kind of man he gonna be. You don't understand, Miss Ruby. His daddy dead and he looking at the man who killed him. He ain't supposed to be looking long.

(King enters from the yard, carrying the machete.)

KING *(Calling loudly)*: Elmore!

TONYA: Come on, King. Come on in the house.

KING: Elmore!

MISTER: Blood for blood.

(Stool Pigeon enters from his house and sits on his steps.)

RUBY: King, don't be starting nothing now.

(King stalks about the yard.)

KING: Elmore!

(Elmore enters from the house.)

ELMORE: What you doing all that hollering for. If you want to see me, come on up and knock on the door and ask for me.

KING: Hey Elmore, the way I see it ... Leroy owed you the fifty dollars. That was man to man. He should have paid you. You say he's my daddy ... I'm gonna pay my daddy's debt. Here goes your fifty dollars.

(King hands Elmore fifty dollars.)

Now we straight on that. But see . . . my name ain't Leroy Slater, Jr. My name is King Hedley II and we got some unfinished business to take care of.

MISTER: Blood for blood, King.

(King takes out a pair of dice.)

KING: The last one cost me seven years. Like I say, this one ain't gonna cost me nothin'. This one gonna be self-defense. Come on . . . let's shoot some crap.

ELMORE: You don't want to shoot no crap with me.

KING: Yeah, I do. Come on, let's play.

RUBY: Come on now, ain't no gambling allowed. You all stop it. Elmore, come on in the house.

ELMORE: You got some money?

KING: I got a pocketful of money. *(He picks up the barbed wire and throws it out of the way)*

MISTER: I want to play. Count me in.

KING: Stay out of this, Mister. You can't get in this game. I wanna play Elmore. *(He stomps on his seeds and clears out the spot to play)* We gonna play man to man. He talking about he always win. Let me see if he win this one.

ELMORE: Somebody got to win. And somebody got to lose. Just like with me and Leroy. You can't all the time say who the winner gonna be.

KING: You ain't gonna win this one. Don't care how many times you won.

MISTER: You the man, King!

RUBY: Come on now. You all stop it.

(Ruby tries to pull Elmore away.)

Tonya, get him.

(Tonya tries to pull King away.)

TONYA: Come on, King. Please. Just come on in the house.

KING: You all get out the way! We doing something here. Shoot twenty dollars.

ELMORE: My dice or yours?

KING: We gonna use mine.

MISTER: Hey King, if you lose your money, I'll back you up. I got some money.

KING: You understand English? Stay out of this.

STOOL PIGEON: You got the Key to the Mountain!

KING: Come on. Shoot twenty. Shoot three to one. Put up your twenty.

(Elmore throws twenty dollars on the ground. King rolls the dice.)

Point four. *(He rolls the dice again)*

MISTER: Blood for blood, King. Be the man!

KING: Six. I'm gonna make that four so you can forget about it. *(He rolls the dice again)* Nine.

STOOL PIGEON: You got the Key to the Mountain. You can go sit on Top of the World.

(King rolls the dice again.)

ELMORE: Seven.

(King throws twenty dollars down on top of Elmore's twenty.)

This ain't but forty dollars. The bet was three to one.

KING: That's what I give you. How much money you got there. Sixty dollars. That's how much you supposed to have.

ELMORE: Twenty of this is mine. That's what I put up.

KING: When you play the lottery, do the state give you back what you played or do they just give you back what you won? Take that sixty dollars and get out my face. Unless you want to make something out of it. You can take it to the limit.

ELMORE: All right. Those are your rules. Those are the rules you wanna play by. Come, let's play. (*He starts to pick up the dice and stops. He rolls the dice*) Seven! (*He starts to pick up the money*)

KING: Naw. That was outside the circle.

ELMORE: What circle? There ain't no circle.

(*King draws a circle with his foot.*)

KING: There is now.

ELMORE: Okay. Now there's a circle. You got everything the way you want it? We gonna play by your rules. You got a circle. Anything else? Now I'm gonna tell you this. Forgiveness is not threefold. I'm gonna roll these dice again. I don't know what's gonna come out of them. I'm taking a chance. I'm willing to take it. You playing a man's game now. Just be sure you know how to play. (*He rolls the dice again*) Eleven!

(*King picks up the dice and looks at them. Elmore starts to pick up the money. King kicks him. Elmore falls to the ground. He starts to get up but King has the machete at his throat.*)

KING: You switched the dice!

TONYA: King! No! No! No!

MISTER: Blood for blood! You got him. Blood for blood!

TONYA: King! No!

(*Unable to harm Elmore, King turns and sticks the machete into the ground.*)

KING: There now . . . you a dead man twice.

STOOL PIGEON: The Key to the Mountain!

(*King turns around to face Stool Pigeon, turning his back on Elmore. Elmore gets up and pulls out his gun. Ruby exits into the house.*)

ELMORE: Turn around, motherfucker!! Turn around!
MISTER: I got your back.
KING: Stay out of this, Mister.
ELMORE: Turn around, let me see your eyes!

(King turns around. Elmore, unable to shoot King, lowers the gun and fires shots into the ground.)

RUBY (Offstage): Elmore!

(King moves toward the house as Ruby enters, firing the derringer that Mister had given him earlier.)

KING: Mama!

(The bullet strikes King in the throat. Tonya screams. King falls on the ground near where the cat is buried. Mister and Tonya go over to King.)

MISTER: King! King! King!
TONYA: Call 911. Call 911.

(Ruby sits down on the ground and starts singing. Elmore goes over to King.)

RUBY (Singing):
    Red sails in the sunset
    Way out on the sea
    Oh carry my loved one
    Bring him home safely to me.

(Stool Pigeon suddenly recognizes that the sacrifice has been made. There is blood on the cat's grave! He is joyous!)

STOOL PIGEON:

> Thy Will! Not man's will! Thy Will!
> You wrote the Beginning and the End!
> Bring down the Fire!
> Stir up the tempest!
> You got the wind in one hand
> And fire in the other!
> Riding a red horse!
> Riding on a black wind!
> The Alpha and the Omega!
> You a bad motherfucker!
> Say I want your best!
> The fatted calf! Not the lean calf.
> The fatted calf!
> Told Abraham You wanted Isaac!
> Say I want your best!
> In the land of plenty
> The storm raging through the land
> Say I want your best!
> From the top of the mountain
> You sent the law!
> I want your best!
> Made the firmament!
> Rolled back the stone!
> I want your best!
> I want Isaac!
> I want the fatted calf!
> Look down the Valley!
> See Him Coming!
> The Redeemer!
> The Conquering Lion of Judea!
> Our Bright and Morning Star!
> I want your best!
> See Him coming!
> We give you our Glory.

We give you our Glory.
We give you our Glory.

(As the lights go down on the scene, the sound of a cat's meow is heard. Fade to black.)

END OF PLAY

AUGUST WILSON is the author of *Gem of the Ocean, Joe Turner's Come and Gone, Ma Rainey's Black Bottom, The Piano Lesson, Seven Guitars, Fences, Two Trains Running, Jitney, King Hedley II* and *Radio Golf*. These works explore the heritage and experience of African Americans, decade-by-decade, over the course of the twentieth century. His plays have been produced at regional theaters across the country and throughout the world, as well as on Broadway.

Mr. Wilson's work has garnered many awards including the Pulitzer Prize for *Fences* (1987) and *The Piano Lesson* (1990); a Tony Award for *Fences*; Great Britain's Olivier Award for *Jitney*; and seven New York Drama Critics Circle Awards for *Ma Rainey's Black Bottom, Fences, Joe Turner's Come and Gone, The Piano Lesson, Two Trains Running, Seven Guitars* and *Jitney*. Additionally, the cast recording of *Ma Rainey's Black Bottom* received a 1985 Grammy Award.

Mr. Wilson has received many fellowships and awards, including Rockefeller and Guggenheim fellowships in playwriting and the Whiting Writers Award. He was awarded a 1999 National Humanities Medal by the President of the United States, and has received numerous honorary degrees from colleges and universities, as well as the only high school diploma ever issued by the Carnegie Library of Pittsburgh.

He is an alumnus of New Dramatists, a member of the American Academy of Arts and Sciences, and in 1995 he was inducted into the American Academy of Arts and Letters.

Mr. Wilson was born and raised in the Hill District of Pittsburgh, and currently makes his home in Seattle. He is the father of two daughters, Sakina Ansari and Azula Carmen Wilson, and is married to costume designer Constanza Romero.